AF486295

Kiprono Mutai
Beyond Borders A Daring Student Athlete

All rights reserved
Copyright © 2024 by **Kiprono Mutai**

No part of this publication may be reproduced, distributed, or transmitted in any form or by any means, including photocopying, recording, or other electronic or mechanical methods, without the prior written permission of the publisher, except in the case of brief quotations embodied in critical reviews and certain other noncommercial uses permitted by copyright law.

Published by Spines
ISBN: 979-8-89383-729-2

BEYOND BORDERS

A DARING STUDENT ATHLETE

KIPRONO MUTAI

This book is a special dedication to my lovely wife and wonderful children—thank you for your unwavering support and love. To my younger brother and his counterpart—your achievements have broken the long chain of what once seemed unachievable. Also, a heartfelt acknowledgment goes out to the exceptional individuals of the central Gash team, Winfred Cyber Cafe. Their remarkable expertise in navigating modern technology has proved invaluable, effectively bridging the gap and connecting me with the broader world. Their skills have fostered communication and collaboration, and their unwavering support is appreciated. To the Fort Lewis Cross Country team and coaches—your guidance and belief in me have lit my path and ensured my success. To the pioneer and a friend who established FLC as a home—your hospitality made my transition to college seamless and welcoming. To Host family—thank you for being my family when I was thousands of miles away from home and to missionary family for going beyond the borders. I also thank the Fort Lewis College community for creating an institution that values diverse cultures and perspectives and fosters an inclusive and equitable environment where students can thrive and develop resilience.

With deepest gratitude,
Kiprono Mutai, MPH

CONTENTS

CHAPTER 1

A FAREWELL AT JOMO KENYATTA AIRPORT

JOMO KENYATTA INTERNATIONAL AIRPORT (JKIA) IN KENYA boasts beautiful and unique scenery. The airport perpetually bustles with heavy traffic, both private and public, as travelers move with purpose. Dragging suitcases around is a common sight, and the atmosphere fills with the warmth of loved ones reuniting, exchanging hugs, and taking selfies or large group photos. However, when I passed through the airport in 2009, I didn't enjoy that luxury. At that time, smartphones with cameras were not prevalent due to technology limitations.

Standing at the airport, ready to embark on a journey to a foreign country, felt like a dream come true. Reflecting on my past, I remembered how the idea of joining a college in America seemed beyond reach, a fantasy scoffed at by many. Such opportunities were often reserved for the wealthy and influential, far from the grasp of ordinary people like me. But thanks to my parents' sacrifices, the unwavering support from siblings and close friends, and a stroke of luck, this moment was now a reality. As I stood there, anticipation mingled with excitement, and tears of joy filled my eyes. This was the culmination of dreams, hard work, and an incredible support system, making the moment not just a milestone, but a celebration of hope and perseverance.

Flanked by a tight-knit group of friends who had become like family during my time in the city, we boarded public transportation together, their presence a comforting send-off as I prepared to depart. As it was our custom to accompany one another during international flights, I knew their support was a testament to the deep bond we shared.

Having made numerous trips to the airport before, I had become well-acquainted with the route, and our previous excursions into the city had always been memorable. Yet, on this day, our focus was singular, and we knew that our final goodbyes would be brief. We had exchanged countless warm embraces in the past, but now it was time for me to continue my journey. With a quick but heartfelt final hug, I proceeded to submit my travel documents for verification and made my way through the security entrance, the familiar faces of my friends slowly receding into the distance as I embarked upon my next adventure.

As I stepped into the lively international airport for the first time, a surge of excitement coursed through me. Thankfully, the attentive air hostesses skillfully guided passengers to their respective airline counters, easing the initial overwhelm of navigating the vast space. Clutching my Qatar Airways ticket, I made my way toward their check-in counter, my emotions a potent cocktail of anticipation and nerves.

The full gravity of the moment hit me, prompting a sudden urge to use the restroom as my mind raced with thoughts of the journey ahead. Amidst the whirlwind of emotions, I was grateful to be beckoned to the next available booth, where a smiling air hostess with quintessential charm greeted me warmly. Her sweet voice immediately set me at ease as she requested my passport and diligently reviewed my documents.

With a friendly congratulations and well-wishes for my upcoming flight, the air hostess handed back my passport and confirmed my travel documents. As my luggage was whisked away to be checked, I took a deep breath, allowing the reality of my imminent departure to fully sink in.

On my back was a small backpack, and in my right hand was a large two-wheel suitcase, fully packed beyond the weight requirement. Inside the suitcase were outfits for various occasions, mostly new, along with scratched, possibly pirated music CDs that I bought from River Road, shower shoes, t-shirts, mirrors—just about everything you could think of. The suitcase's weight exceeded international requirements, and I was advised by the airport staff to transfer some items to my backpack.

"No rush, just take your time and let me know when you're ready," she told me. I was used to people jumping the line or going ahead if you weren't ready, but here they genuinely meant it. After redistributing the weight, I needed to weigh the suitcase again. Even though I was sure it was still overweight, the staff member looked the other way and only asked if I had any liquids or flammable items in my bag. I replied no. The suitcase was tagged and sent off, and I was instructed to proceed to customs and clearance.

I felt lighter and unburdened, now only carrying my passport, boarding pass, and backpack after checking in my luggage. As I waited to be cleared by Kenyan customs and clearance, my mind raced, trying to recall if anything in my backpack could be considered flammable. I suddenly remembered a bottle of methylated spirit, a common antiseptic back home, which I had been advised to bring since it wasn't sold in America. Thoughts of how to dispose of the bottle swirled in my head, mingled with anxiety about the horror stories of passengers being arrested for carrying prohibited items. Just then, I saw someone walk toward the bathroom after clearing customs, and I felt a wave of relief. My documents were verified shortly after, my passport stamped with "exit JKIA" and the date, and I was finally free to proceed.

Following check-in and customs clearance, all travelers, especially those boarding a flight to the United States, underwent more rigorous security checks. This included passing through metal detectors and having their carry-on bags screened by X-ray machines. It was finally my turn for the third screening, and I was becoming accustomed to the process. I placed my carry-on bag on the conveyor belt, where it passed through a machine capable of seeing its contents. The process was quick, and there was nothing unusual in my bag. Earlier, I had poured the methylated spirit down the sink in the bathroom, ensuring I had no prohibited items. Watching uniformed security personnel supervise the entire process was both fascinating and reassuring. I felt a sense of security, knowing I was one step closer to boarding the plane and beginning a new chapter in my life.

As I looked out the window in the waiting area, the bustling activities on the tarmac unfolded before me like a well-choreographed performance. A sense of excitement bubbled within me as I tried to guess which plane, I would board. The anticipation made my heart race a little faster. I scanned the lineup of aircraft, noting their colors, logos, and sizes, imagining which one might be mine. Each plane seemed to hold the promise of adventure, and I couldn't help but speculate about its destination and what stories it might carry. The thought of boarding one of these magnificent machines, soaring above the clouds to a new place, filled me with childlike wonder. Planes of various sizes and colors were parked at their gates, with workers efficiently moving luggage and cargo. They skillfully maneuvered carts and containers, ensuring each piece of baggage found its way to the correct aircraft. In the distance, planes were taking off and landing with remarkable precision. The sight of a plane gracefully lifting off the ground, and ascending into the sky, was mesmerizing. Equally captivating was the steady descent of incoming flights, touching down smoothly on the runway. The rhythmic hum of engines and the coordinated movements of ground staff created a dynamic and vibrant scene, a testament to the intricate operations of air travel.

Queuing for the final checkpoint before boarding the plane to Doha's Qatar International Airport, I found myself awash in a sea of emotions. An intoxicating blend of anticipation and anxiety pulsed through me as I observed the diverse array of passengers lining up in designated groups.

Admittedly, my lack of familiarity with the system didn't faze me—all I yearned for was to board the aircraft and begin my journey. The soft murmur of various languages filled the air as travelers presented their passports for verification, each individual contributing to the rich tapestry of humanity gathered at the gate. Driven by my desire to appear knowledgeable and self-assured, I attentively watched the proceedings, a habit ingrained in me from my school days.

As I approached the counter, a smartly dressed crew greeted me with a radiant smile, warmth, and tangible kindness. She extended her congratulations on my impending adventure to America, and I reciprocated her grin, my heart fluttering wildly with a mixture of trepidation and excitement. The moment she returned my verified documents, a surge of realization dawned upon me. I was mere moments away from boarding the plane and embarking on a new, transformative chapter of my life.

CHAPTER 2

SOARING INTO NEW HORIZONS

AT THAT YOUNGER AGE, I FOUND MYSELF BOARDING A PLANE for the very first time, struggling to believe that this long-awaited moment had finally arrived. While I was accustomed to public transportation, the atmosphere inside the aircraft was unlike anything I had encountered before. The air hostesses, elegantly attired in maroon uniforms, appeared as if they had stepped right out of a billboard. Their speech, although carrying an unfamiliar accent, was remarkably easy to comprehend. With my boarding pass in hand, I ventured further into the plane, only to be met with a beaming smile from one of the attendants.

I handed over my boarding pass, and the air hostess glanced at it before pointing me toward my seat. As I walked to sit down, a wave of excitement washed over me—a feeling I'd never experienced before. At that age, I found myself inside a plane, struggling to believe that this long-awaited moment had finally arrived. In an attempt to affirm the reality of the situation, I pinched myself, a traditional way of testing my existence, feeling the pain, and acknowledging the truth of the experience.

Earlier, as I approached the doorstep, a smartly dressed crew member greeted me with a radiant smile. "Good afternoon, boy?" she inquired, her warmth radiating in her voice. Reflexively, I responded, "Good afternoon, madam," a phrase ingrained in me from school and one that had never failed to garner appreciation from working-class citizens back home. Her genuine smile took me aback, as such displays of friendliness towards strangers were a rarity in my culture and typically implied familiarity, eccentricity, or fondness. At that moment, I couldn't help but ponder whether her smile was part of her professional duties or if, perhaps, it was the culture. As I settled into my seat, I found myself continually reflecting on the interaction, allowing the novelty and excitement of the experience to sweep me.

I wished I had a smartphone or a video camera to capture the moment, to create a story I could share with my family, who were likely imagining how everything was going for me. Glancing around, I didn't recognize any faces, not even any new friends, since I was never comfortable staring at people. Back home, I'd watched many Nigerian movies about some characters, who often gawked at new surroundings with their mouths wide open. This made me smile as I realized how different my own experience was becoming, full of new and unfamiliar adventures.

My seat was located towards the back of the plane, and to my delight, it was a window seat—just as I had always imagined. I didn't want to miss a thing. Having often watched planes fly above the city, I never dreamed that one day I would be one of the passengers soaring above it. Holding my backpack, I initially rested it on the floor, but it quickly became uncomfortable. Observing a fellow passenger confidently place a much larger bag in the overhead compartment, I didn't hesitate. Standing up with newfound confidence, I opened the compartment, put my backpack inside, and closed it securely. It felt empowering. Back in the city, bus drivers would often take your luggage and stuff it somewhere; sometimes, you'd never see it again. If you did, it might be torn, dusty, squeezed, and leaking—especially if you were carrying a two-liter milk container from your village. This moment on the plane felt like a small triumph, a sign that I was stepping into a new world of experiences.

Seated in my row were two other passengers, clearly not locals, and likely heading home. They looked wealthy, a conclusion I arrived at based on their attire—a skill I honed while hanging out with my friends in town. Both of them were quiet, eyes closed most of the time, leaving me to wonder what was going on in their heads. I tried not to look around too much; the last thing I wanted was to scare myself. Everyone's heard stories of plane hijackings, and some passengers, based on appearances alone, could easily pull you into those movie scenes. Maybe I had spent too long in the village, but I convinced myself that this was just how the world looked now.

I also had the chance to glimpse at the two pilots seated in front, smartly dressed in uniforms just like on TV. Back in elementary school, many kids talked about wanting to be pilots—a dream so big that it would invite laughter if you mentioned it. I never aspired to be a pilot; instead, I chose the more achievable dream of becoming a teacher, a goal that wouldn't be scoffed at. Aiming a bit higher, I imagined myself as a high school teacher or lecturer. As I settled into my seat, I found myself comparing the real plane to the images I had in my mind, checking off what was true.

It was at this moment that I recalled an experience shared by one of my school teachers. She had told us about a candy given to all passengers at the beginning of the flight. Thinking it was just regular candy, she saved it for later. However, as the plane took off, she began experiencing an excruciating headache due to the elevation change, feeling as if her whole brain was going to fall apart—an unprecedented sensation for her. After getting the attention of the crew, she was advised to munch on the hard candy sublingually, and everything was fine.

As I sat there, I realized that everything I had watched in movies, read about, or heard in stories was now coming into play. This was my reality, and the excitement of these new experiences made the moment even more memorable. Immediately when I saw one of the air hostesses passing out what seemed to be old-school candies, maybe even bubble gum, I made sure to grab one and eat it, determined to avoid any potential sickness and the drama that could come with it.

It didn't take long before the plane was full and flagged to depart. The engine sounds grew louder, signaling that we were about to take off. I kept looking out through the tiny window, ensuring no engineers were pointing out discrepancies with the plane. Identifying engineers was hard since they all wore reflective jackets, but I kept an eye out for anyone wielding a huge adjustable spanner. Thankfully, everything seemed normal. The weather was perfect; it was around 3:00 p.m., and the sky was clear, promising beautiful views. The seatbelt sign illuminated, and flight attendants walked around, making sure everyone was strapped in, comfortable, and had their electronics turned off.

I flew on the Qatar Airways A350-1000 from Nairobi to Doha, a marvel of modern aviation. The aircraft boasts a sleek, streamlined design with its iconic white fuselage gilded with the burgundy Qatar Airways logo and branding. This advanced jet features a spacious and quiet cabin, designed for comfort with wider seats and higher ceilings. I settled into my window seat, a choice I made to ensure I could get a glimpse of how the ground looked from high up in the sky.

The anticipation of seeing the world from this new perspective filled me with excitement. I eagerly awaited the breathtaking views and the unique experience of watching the landscape transform as we ascended into the clouds. The plane's state-of-the-art capabilities include advanced aerodynamics and a carbon-fiber fuselage, contributing to improved fuel efficiency and a smoother ride.

The A350-1000 I was on was equipped with the latest in-flight entertainment systems, offering passengers a vast selection of movies, TV shows, and music on high-resolution screens. Designed for efficient long-haul flights, the A350-1000 ensured a pleasant and luxurious travel experience, making my journey from Nairobi to Doha both comfortable and memorable.

When the captain welcomed everyone on board, providing details about the length of the flight, speed, and altitude, a mix of excitement and nervousness filled me. Hearing his calm and reassuring voice made the experience feel more real and official. As he described the journey ahead, I marveled at the idea of flying at such incredible speeds and altitudes. The captain's closing words, "sit back, relax, and enjoy the flight," offered a sense of comfort and anticipation. It was a surreal moment, knowing I was about to embark on an adventure that I had only dreamed of, and his words helped me feel at ease, ready to embrace every aspect of this new experience.

The plane taxied to a long tarmac painted black and white, which I recognized as the runway after seeing at least two planes take off from it. We paused there for a few minutes as the engines roared to their maximum, their power resonating in my inner ears. Suddenly, the plane began moving, accelerating to a breakneck speed that far surpassed any vehicle I'd ever seen. The world outside blurred as we raced down the runway, and then, with a smooth, almost imperceptible lift, we were airborne. The sudden quiet and calmness confirmed that we were flying. A loud bang outside briefly startled me, but seeing the other passengers unfazed reassured me that everything was under control.

As the plane ascended, I relaxed and experienced the most wonderful feeling ever. No longer would I have to deal with the noise and traffic of Nairobi CBD or the constant worry of being misled by people pretending to sell some herbal medicine that can cure every illness you can imagine in the city headquarters? As the plane took off, the scenery below unfolded like a vivid tapestry. The sprawling expanse of the airport, with its multiple runways and busy terminals, gradually shrank beneath us. Beyond the airport grounds, the bustling traffic of Nairobi's highways came into view, cars and buses moving like tiny dots in organized chaos.

The landscape was a patchwork of green and brown, dotted with clusters of buildings that made up the city's diverse neighborhoods. In the distance, the Nairobi National Park was visible, a unique juxtaposition of wilderness against the urban backdrop. I could make out herds of zebras and giraffes roaming freely in their natural habitat, offering a striking contrast to the modernity of the airport and city. As we climbed higher, the horizon expanded, revealing the rolling hills and savannas that define the region's geography. The scene was a beautiful blend of nature and human development, encapsulating the essence of Nairobi.

Looking down at the city, tears of joy streamed down my face. I couldn't hold them back as I thought about how far I had come, the challenges I faced, and the sacrifices my parents and siblings made to support me. I vowed to always think about them, be there for them, and repay their love. I knew I would miss my family, the food, and the culture.

As the familiar landscape faded away, I realized lunch would be somewhere else, and it was hard to predict when I would next enjoy my mother's home-cooked meals. Being so close to my siblings, sharing everything in common, taking each other's advice, and praying for one another was going to be missed dearly. Leaving all that behind was bittersweet, and their smiles reassuring me that everything would be alright played over in my mind. Their last hugs lingered with me, knowing I would be gone for more than a year, unsure if I would see them all again. Convincing myself that I made the right choice, I hoped to shine a light upon them in the future.

Most of the passengers appeared to be business people and high-class citizens, likely traveling to Qatar for visits or returning home. I imagined. I noticed there were fewer than three students on the plane, which filled me with pride, knowing I had earned my place here. My travel documents were safe with me the entire time in a separate plastic folder. I made sure to carry them personally in case I lost my luggage or forgot it due to the excitement. At least with my travel documentation, I could still get to college even without my items. This precaution reassured me, allowing me to fully savor the journey ahead.

As I sat down, relaxed and full of excitement, I couldn't quite believe how far I had come. The memories of a few months ago were still vivid in my mind: plucking tea, feeding the farm animals, and doing other chores that had filled my days. It was surreal to think that I might not be doing those things again anytime soon. The pain of leaving my family behind was always there, and I couldn't stop imagining when I would return to see them. Yet, the inspiration from my parents and the community reminded me that I was on the right path. Deep in my thoughts, I kept coming back to reality and telling myself, "This is awesome."

It took a few minutes, and the plane was already up around 30,000 feet in the air. The pilot announced that the plane was at a good altitude and that it was okay to take off the seatbelts and use electronics for those who had cellphones and computers, a luxury I didn't have. I was unsure whether to stand up and walk around or just sit there. I was afraid I might not find my way back, and I was not sure if they had bathrooms inside or if they were located somewhere else. Based on what I heard in the past, most people said bathrooms were inside the plane, but I guess they never knew they were referred to as lavatories. After seeing a few people walk around, I decided to give it a try. One passenger was seated beside me, and I had to excuse myself to get out. We hadn't spoken to each other since the plane took off.

I stood up, excused myself, and walked towards the back of the plane. It looked like a kitchen area, and it smelled different but pleasant. Unsure of where the bathrooms were located, I eventually spotted them. One was occupied, and the other was vacant. Not knowing exactly what to do, I decided to hang around casually, pretending I had no intention of using the bathroom until the next person showed up. Within less than a minute, an older gentleman arrived and asked if I was waiting. I told him I was fine, and he entered the tiny room. As he opened the door, I quickly scanned inside to confirm it was the right place.

When the other door opened, I entered confidently, trying to look as if I were one of the crew. Inside the bathroom, I saw the seatbelt sign light up. I immediately hurried back to my seat, buckled up, and settled down. However, even with the seatbelt sign still on, I noticed some people walking up and down the aisle. Seeing this, I unbuckled my seatbelt and started playing with the LCD screen in front of me since the urge to use the bathroom had disappeared.

At first, I was tempted to fiddle with the screen, but the fear of breaking it and ending up with a bill I couldn't afford kept my curiosity in check. With about $250 in my pocket and a long journey ahead, I was cautious not to add "broken screen" to my travel expenses. Despite partially studying Geography in high school for two years, I quickly got the hang of the navigation system, figuring out our arrival time like a seasoned traveler—at least in my mind. Soon, I was jamming to some tunes, including hits from my favorite South African reggae legend, Lucky Dube. I remembered the tragic news of his untimely death; the radio stations had mourned him with an all-night marathon of his music. Now, here I was, savoring his hard-to-find tracks on repeat. If only my Geography teacher could see me now, mastering technology and geography on the go while grooving to reggae beats!

The afternoon flight served lunch, and I was thrilled to finally taste airplane food, having heard so many good things about it. There was no hand washing, but a crew member handed out moist towels. I had no clue what to do with it, so I pretended to admire the view out the window, sneakily peeking to see what the seasoned travelers did. One passenger, clearly a pro, started wiping his hands, so I followed suit, even wiping my dry lips and face. Then came the hot meal, which looked like beef—I wasn't sure, but it was delicious. Not being a big eater, I was quickly satisfied. As a Kenyan fresh off the farm, I asked for milk and got a treat: packed Ultra Heat-Treated milk, a rare luxury back home. We usually get milk straight from the cow, which can be an adventure if the cow decides to swat tsetse flies, sending the milk jug flying. The meal ended with what they called dessert—chocolate, which I tasted for the second time. It was so good I wanted to ask for more, but I held back, fearing they might just hand me the whole stash!

The estimated time of the flight was about six hours, it felt like an eternity for a first-time flyer used to short, rough public transport rides. Unlike the cramped and uncomfortable bus rides with loud music, the flight offered assigned seating, ample legroom, air-conditioning, and my earpiece, which I kept as a souvenir. Two movies and reggae music kept me entertained, making the long journey enjoyable and comfortable. With a full belly and bottled water, I felt reassured that I was headed in the right direction.

The pilot's calm voice came over the intercom, announcing that the flight would begin its descent and we would be landing in about 20 minutes. He reminded all passengers to fasten their seatbelts and the crew to return to their seats. For a first-time traveler like me, the announcement brought a mix of excitement and nervousness. The reality of the journey's end and the anticipation of what lay ahead filled me with a thrilling sense of adventure. I quickly buckled my seatbelt, feeling a flutter in my stomach as the plane started its gentle descent, marking the final leg of this unforgettable experience.

The plane descended, and the ground became visible, revealing a stunning view of buildings and streets, a sight I had only seen in movies. As we approached the runway, I reminded myself that this was happening. The plane landed safely, and I was fascinated by the size of the airport and the bustling activity—bigger planes, larger runways, and trains and buses ferrying passengers to various gates.

The air hostess's cheerful voice came over the intercom, announcing our arrival in Doha, Qatar. She thanked us for flying with them and reminded us to check that we had all our personal belongings before disembarking. Her instructions were clear and courteous, urging everyone to double-check the overhead compartments and the areas around their seats for any luggage or items they might have brought on board. As the plane taxied to the gate, her warm tone added a sense of calm and order, ensuring that everyone was prepared for a smooth and organized exit from the aircraft.

As the plane came to a stop at the gate, the crew began guiding us with practiced efficiency. Passengers were instructed to disembark row by row, ensuring an orderly exit. We gathered our belongings from the overhead compartments and under the seats, double-checking to make sure nothing was left behind. The air hostesses and stewards, stationed at intervals along the aisle, offered warm smiles and polite farewells, directing us towards the customs. For those with connecting flights, clear instructions were given over the intercom, detailing the location of transfer desks and gates, and advising them to follow the signs for connecting flights. Their assistance and clear guidance made the transition smooth and stress-free, allowing me to proceed with confidence toward the next part of our journey.

CHAPTER 3

DOHA LAYOVER

As I proceeded to customs, I got my passport stamped and verified my next destination. Passengers flying to the U.S., about ten or more of us, were set aside for an overnight stay before our next morning flight. Confirming this on my boarding pass, I waited with the others for transportation. We stood by a door that magically opened with a sensor as people approached, something I had never seen before. Curious, I tried it myself, and it opened! Stepping outside, I felt a blast of intense summer heat, over 100 degrees Fahrenheit, a stark contrast to the weather back home.

Stepping into a foreign land for the first time since graduating high school, I felt my initial fear dissipate, replaced by a sense of perfect timing. Embracing the diverse world around me, I marveled at the variety of dress codes—from the beauty of headscarves to the allure of fully covered faces, and the unexpected charm of men in skirt-like attire. The people I encountered were respectful and gentle, traits that quickly rubbed off on me as I navigated this new environment.

As I strolled through the airport, I couldn't help but notice that everyone seemed to keep a respectful distance from one another. Adopting this new custom, I found it surprisingly enjoyable to blend in with the local culture and adopt their courteous ways. In this unfamiliar place, I was delighted to discover that learning from others could be a simple yet enriching experience, allowing me to appreciate the unique beauty of our diverse world.

A sleek black minivan, possibly brand new with spotless leather seats and cool air conditioning, whisked me away to a five-star hotel in Doha for the night. The excitement of having a full row to myself was exhilarating. Gazing out the window, I admired the skillful driver who expertly navigated the bustling city streets. The view outside was mesmerizing, a mix of modern skyscrapers and beautifully lit avenues. The entire experience felt surreal, a stark contrast to my usual travels, filling me with anticipation for the journey ahead.

The minivan gracefully came to a halt in front of an elegant hotel, accompanied by an assortment of high-end vehicles that appeared as if they had just rolled off the assembly line. An array of vibrant colors and foreign license plates, reminiscent of scenes from the silver screen, caught my eye. As I observed the stylish guests strolling in and out of the luxurious establishment, I couldn't help but feel a surge of excitement for the promise of even greater experiences that awaited me on this extraordinary adventure.

The vibrant energy of this upscale setting served as a captivating reminder that the best was yet to come, inspiring a sense of anticipation for the remarkable moments that were still to unfold throughout my incredible journey.

Checking in at the hotel reserved by the airline was an adventure in itself. I handed over my passport at the front desk in exchange for a keycard and was informed that my room was on the upper floor. The thought of figuring out how to get there added to the excitement. Navigating the hotel's elevators, I pressed the button for the 20th floor and watched the numbers light up as I ascended. The ride-up offered a brief but thrilling preview of the luxury awaiting me, and I couldn't wait to see my room.

Upon arriving on the floor, I was relieved to find my room number conveniently indicated on the keycard. Holding a keycard for the first time, I felt a mix of curiosity and excitement about unlocking the door, despite being unsure of the exact process. Standing at the door, I meticulously verified the room number three times, ensuring it matched the number on my keycard, before proceeding to attempt to unlock it. After several unsuccessful tries, a kind gentleman, who seemed to be traveling with his wife, offered assistance. He showed me the correct way to insert the keycard, explaining that the arrow should face down. Grateful, I thanked him and decided to test my new knowledge. I closed the door and tried again, and boom, the door opened smoothly like magic.

I proceeded to enter the room and immediately noticed it was dark. Flicking the light switch up and down countless times did nothing. Thinking of my helpful next-door neighbor, I rushed to his door, which was still open. Without hesitation, he followed me to my room and did the magic again, inserting the keycard into a device by the light switch. Initially, I thought it was just for show, perhaps a peephole. With the lights on, I finally proceeded to check out the room.

The kindness extended to me by a total stranger was a powerful reminder that, regardless of our diverse backgrounds, humanity is inherently good. This moment of unexpected assistance reinforced my belief in the universal bond that connects us all as descendants of a shared ancestry. Embracing this lesson, I made a solemn vow to pay it forward, spreading the same kindness and compassion to others.

For someone not accustomed to such gracious gestures, the experience etched a lasting smile upon my face—a testament to the profound impact that even a simple act of kindness can have on the human spirit.

It took me a while to settle down because the room was perfect, just like in most movies. I kept thinking that it must have been all the money I paid the airline that I was spending. Everything seemed different and perfect in a certain way. The bed was exceptional, and the room boasted a 40-inch flatscreen TV and unique decorations that added to its beauty. It was hot, and I wanted to take a shower. I jumped in and almost burned myself because I turned on the hot water. Not wanting to seem crazy by asking around how to work the shower, I figured it out and experienced my first warm shower. I was used to showering with other boys in the river with cold water, no privacy, and always rushing for fear of women—or worse, my mother—walking down to fetch water. I missed it, but this shower wiped those memories away.

As the room gradually cooled under the influence of the unfamiliar air conditioning, my gaze fell upon the thermostat mounted on the wall. Its presence, however, did little to assuage my hesitation—the fear of inadvertently causing damage or worsening the conditions loomed large. After all, my upbringing had instilled a harsh lesson: break something, and you'd either be faced with a financial penalty or, worse still, physical punishment. With these consequences firmly ingrained in my mind, I opted to leave the thermostat untouched, resigned to let the room temperature remain as it was.

Feeling like an expert, I walked around and even made a phone call back home, letting my father know where I was and how awesome everything was. It was a good feeling. I didn't want to stay on the phone for long because I was used to postpaid phones that were expensive to maintain, and any conversation longer than two minutes would cost a lot of money. Since departing Jomo Kenyatta International Airport, I had not had the opportunity to speak my native language until that brief call. By this time, my mouth was aching to speak it, but there was no one around to converse with. It felt strange, yearning to express myself freely without any barriers, yet finding no outlet. This longing highlighted the onset of a new reality, where my familiar words and expressions were confined to memory, and I began to sense that this was merely the beginning of a journey that would challenge my linguistic and cultural comfort zones. However, I was up for the challenge.

I was starting to get hungry and wasn't sure where to get food. I kept looking around, hoping some magic electric tray would deliver it. That didn't happen, so I decided to call the front desk and inquire about dinner. I finally made my way down to the mezzanine floor as instructed. In the buffet-style room, I was unsure where to start. Luckily, I met another Kenyan frequent traveler returning from the U.S. He guided me on what was good and invited me to sit with him. A talkative man in his 40s, he shared stories about the U.S., assuring me I'd enjoy it and meet good people. When I mentioned being a student-athlete, he congratulated me, noting how hard it was to get a sponsorship. We eventually parted ways, and he wished me well, encouraging me to bring back good things. Hearing this from someone experienced with a foreign country made me happy.

After dinner, I made my way back to the room which was easier to find this time round given my early experience. My belly was full and satisfied, not sleepy I jumped on to a queen bed size, I did not even occupy a quarter of the bed. The queen-sized bed in this elegant hotel room beckons with its plush comfort, meticulously ornamented with crisp, luxurious linens. The soft, inviting mattress ensures a restful slumber, while an array of fluffy pillows offers ample support. An exquisitely tailored duvet envelops the bed, adding both warmth and a touch of refined sophistication. The headboard, a masterpiece of craftsmanship, showcases intricate designs that whisper tales of grandeur and elegance. As a testament to the hotel's attention to detail, the bed is perfectly centered within the room, flanked by sophisticated nightstands that support graceful lamps, illuminating the space with a warm, soothing glow. Every aspect of this refined retreat radiates an undeniable allure, promising an unparalleled sanctuary for rest and rejuvenation.

Gripping the remote firmly, I decided to switch on the television. As the screen flickered to life, I found myself tuning into a news broadcast delivered in an unfamiliar language. Despite the linguistic barrier, the coverage managed to captivate my attention, offering a compelling glimpse into the world through the lens of another culture's perspective.

As the events of the day gradually caught up with me, the tranquility of the surroundings lulled me into a state of deep relaxation. My memories of drifting off to sleep remain hazy, yet the profound sense of restorative slumber I experienced stands as a testament to the unparalleled comfort offered by the hotel. If allowed to review the establishment, I would undoubtedly award it the highest accolade—a resounding five-star rating.

CHAPTER 4

DEPARTING DOHA, QATAR

My next flight was at 6:00 a.m., and I was awake and ready by 5:00 a.m., fearing I might oversleep. At half past five, I received a wake-up call reminding me to head to the front desk for my ride to the airport, which was just a few minutes away. A different minivan was waiting in front of the hotel. After checking out and getting my passport back, it was time to go. I boarded the minivan, feeling energetic and ready for the next flight. The airport was only a few miles away, and we arrived within minutes. The driver, a professional with years of experience, impressed me with his hospitality and driving skills, just like the previous driver. Upon arrival, all passengers and their luggage got off the bus, and airport officials directed us where to go for check-in.

All passengers lined up in order, and I noticed more Americans this time, confirming that we were heading to the same destination. Security was tight yet orderly, with everyone following directions efficiently. When my turn came, I approached the counter and handed over my passport and accompanying documents, including my boarding pass and admission letter to justify my reason for traveling. Now accustomed to the process, I smoothly followed the instructions and proceeded to the next checkpoint.

The security at Jomo Kenyatta International Airport was minimal, yet up to standard. However, the thorough checkpoint for U.S.-bound passengers was a different story. The directions and instructions were clear: shoes off and all bags in a bin. It was easier for me since I had only one bag and no electronics. After passing through the scanner, my bag was opened, and every valuable item, including large Kiwi black shoe polish, Vaseline, lotion, and a mirror, was thrown on the floor. I tried to stay calm despite having spent a lot of money on these products. One tall, no-nonsense agent with blue gloves handled my items with the precision of someone who had been doing this for decades. I learned a lesson but stood firm and let them do their job. Though disheartened, I moved on and proceeded to the next gate, ready to continue my journey.

It didn't take long before we boarded the flight. Everything was in order, similar to before, although the final queue to verify boarding passes and passports took longer due to the large number of passengers. The airport crew, professional and helpful, always smiled and waved, a habit I began to pick up. Around me were various passengers, some returning home to the United States, others traveling for business, and a few students like me. I met another Kenyan student during check-in, he was also joining a college in the U.S. His fluent Swahili hinted at his academic excellence, but here we were in the same situation. I proceeded to board the plane, ready for the next leg of my journey.

My plane this time round was an Airbus A380 Qatar airplane. A marvel of modern aviation, featuring a spacious seating arrangement with a capacity of over 500 passengers, awaited me. It was nice, comfortable, and something I couldn't wait to talk about. The flight was long, and we had breakfast, lunch, and dinner, making it feel like a 16-hour journey. Everything was smooth and well-organized. I became more social and familiar with the protocols, and strangers' smiles and waves made me feel welcome. I adjusted well from the previous flight, confidently using help buttons and asking for snacks. The food was good, though I missed my usual chai, and I started to get a light headache from the lack of caffeine.

The seating was divided into three classes: First, Business, and Economy, each offering ample legroom and comfort. If you're wondering, I was in economy class, which is perfect for students on a budget who just want to reach their destination. It was comfortable, and once again, I had a window seat. The view from the window added to the excitement of my journey, making the long flight more enjoyable and giving me a chance to see the world from above. Equipped with state-of-the-art technology, it included individual entertainment systems, Wi-Fi, and adjustable lighting. The flight attendants were exceptionally hospitable, consistently offering smiles, assistance, and refreshments throughout the flight. The pilots, dressed in crisp uniforms, exuded professionalism and confidence, ensuring a smooth and reliable flight experience. The A380's advanced engineering allows it to handle long-haul flights with ease, making the journey comfortable and efficient for all passengers.

In the seat, there was a blanket and a pillow, promising relief and comfort. Dressed in blue jeans and a red t-shirt, I sat down, looking through the window with excitement. The plane was ready for takeoff, and the captain's instructions were given. Familiar with the drill, I fastened my seatbelt, eager for our next landing in the United States. The massive plane, with its large wings and engines, slowly moved to the runway. Filled with anticipation, I explored the plane's amenities, finding a safety manual I briefly glanced at before focusing on the photo and other in-flight services.

As we settled into our seats and prepared for take-off in Qatar, the pilot's voice came over the intercom with a warm and professional tone. "Ladies and gentlemen, this is your captain speaking. Welcome aboard this flight from Doha to Washington. We are currently awaiting final clearance from air traffic control and will be taking off shortly. For your safety, please ensure that your seatbelts are securely fastened, your seat backs are in the upright position, and your tray tables are stowed."

He continued with detailed instructions, "All carry-on luggage should be securely placed in the overhead compartments or under the seat in front of you. Please turn off all electronic devices or switch them to airplane mode at this time. Smoking is prohibited for the duration of the flight. In the event of an emergency, follow the illuminated signs and crew instructions."

After covering the safety procedures, he welcomed us warmly, "We are expecting a smooth flight today with a cruising altitude of 35,000 feet and an average speed of 560 miles per hour. The weather along our route looks favorable, and we anticipate an on-time arrival. Our flight attendants will be coming through the cabin shortly to ensure everyone is comfortable and to provide a demonstration of the safety features of this aircraft. We thank you for choosing to fly with us today, and we hope you have a pleasant journey."

The pilot's thorough instructions and reassuring tone set the stage for a safe and comfortable flight, as the excitement of the journey ahead began to build.

As the Airbus A380 prepared for takeoff, I felt a surge of excitement. The plane's engines roared to life, and it began its gradual acceleration down the runway. Looking out the window, I saw the expansive airport grounds, with sleek, modern buildings and well-organized runways shrinking as we gained altitude. The sensation of climbing was exhilarating, and I watched in awe as the landscape below transformed, buildings becoming tiny dots and roads turning into thin lines. The plane ascended smoothly, and I felt a mix of thrill and anticipation as we soared higher into the sky, knowing that the next landing would be in the United States.

As soon as the plane stabilized and the seatbelt sign went off, I settled in, feeling more comfortable than before. I reached for the LCD screen display to check the flight distance and hours ahead. It was a long journey, so I decided to watch a series of movies and TV shows. When breakfast was served, my growing hunger and caffeine withdrawal made me eager for the meal. I chose the first option offered, enjoying a satisfying new dish and a cup of hot tea. Seated beside me were two other travelers of different nationalities, both seemingly far from home, reminding me that I wasn't alone on this journey of hope and disbelief.

The flight lasted about 16 hours, spanning an entire day and a few more hours. As time passed, my memories of home began to fade, replaced by thoughts of my future and the pursuit of a quality education. The dream felt increasingly real with each passing second, filled with hope. Familiar with the plane, I confidently took bathroom breaks, reciting my seat number to avoid any mishaps. Lunch came, and I ordered the offered meal, a traditional dish with unfamiliar spices that was deliciously spicy. The utensils were classy, and the dessert cake was a treat. I savored every bite, feeling more optimistic with each meal.

Ordering soda with every meal was a new delight, a luxury not common back home, where soda was considered a treat for the wealthy. I enjoyed this newfound privilege, asking for more cans of soda, a request that was never denied. Watching my neighbor frequently order snacks, I embraced the habit of enjoying the variety of foods available, hoping it wasn't adding to the cost of the flight.

Wine and alcoholic beverages, forbidden back home, didn't even cross my mind to order. I observed the passenger next to me sip what seemed like red wine, a scene reminiscent of Nigerian and American movies. This entire experience, from the unique meals to the constant supply of soda and the sophisticated ambiance, made the long journey enjoyable and filled with new experiences, making me feel like a frequent flyer.

During the flight, we experienced a brief period of turbulence. The plane shook and jolted, causing a few moments of anxiety among the passengers. The seatbelt sign was promptly turned on, and the flight attendants quickly reassured everyone to remain seated and secure. Despite the initial fright, the turbulence didn't last long. Within minutes, the plane stabilized, and the journey resumed its smooth course. The incident was soon forgotten as passengers returned to their in-flight activities, feeling reassured by the crew's calm and professional response.

Dinner time while flying was a delightful experience. The meal service was handled by professional flight attendants who moved gracefully through the aisles, offering a variety of delicious dishes. The food was well-prepared, with options catering to different tastes and dietary needs. I enjoyed a flavorful main course, accompanied by fresh salads and warm Italian bread. For dessert, there was a selection of pastries and fruits. Drinks were plentiful, including juices, soft drinks, and tea, all served with a smile. Dining high up in the sky felt like a gourmet experience, adding to the overall enjoyment of the flight.

As the flight neared its end, the captain announced that we would be landing at Seattle International Airport in about twenty minutes. A wave of excitement and anticipation washed over me as I reflected on how far I had come and the new journey that awaited me. Despite being tired and sleepy from short naps during the flight, the thought of finally reaching my destination filled me with renewed energy. I marveled at the progress I had made, from leaving my home country to navigating airports and long flights, all leading up to this moment. The lights of Washington began to twinkle below, each one a beacon of the opportunities and experiences that lay ahead. My heart raced with a mix of nervousness and exhilaration as I thought about the new chapter in my life that was about to begin, full of hopes, dreams, and the promise of a bright future.

As we approached Seattle International Airport, the captain announced our imminent landing, and a ripple of excitement spread through the cabin. Flight attendants handed out customs forms to all non-U.S. citizens, and soon, passengers were busy filling them out, asking each other questions about the details. "Do you know what to put for this section?" I heard someone ask behind me. "Is this where we list the items we're bringing in?" another passenger inquired, turning to their seatmate for clarification. My curiosity piqued, I leaned toward the window, eager to catch my first glimpse of America. The chatter and activity added to the anticipation, making the moment even more thrilling.

The aerial view was nothing short of breathtaking. The city sprawled out beneath us, with perfectly organized buildings and roads that offered a blend of advanced infrastructure and scenic routes that looked like meticulously drawn diagrams. The sight of countless vehicles moving along the roads affirmed that I had finally arrived in the United States. My heart swelled with a mix of relief, excitement, and a touch of disbelief. The reality of my dream coming true was almost overwhelming. The exhaustion from the long journey momentarily faded as I absorbed the magnificent view below.

The organized beauty of the cityscape and the sense of bustling life filled me with a renewed sense of purpose. The streets below were lined with orderly rows of trees, their green canopies providing a striking contrast to the concrete and glass structures that defined the skyline. Cars moved in well-coordinated patterns, and the sight of people going about their daily routines added to the dynamic energy of the scene. Everything looked exactly as I had imagined, with iconic landmarks standing tall and recognizable, confirming that I had indeed arrived in a place of opportunity and adventure. The blend of urban sophistication and natural beauty was equally mesmerizing, and I felt a deep sense of excitement and anticipation. There was no doubt in my mind that I was in the right place, ready to embark on this new chapter of my life. The promise of new experiences, learning, and personal growth filled me with optimism, and I couldn't wait to step off the plane and immerse myself in this vibrant, new world.

CHAPTER 5

A CLOSE CALL

WE GOT OFF THE PLANE AFTER OVER 15 HOURS OF FLYING. The time zone had changed, and it was afternoon when we landed. With a connecting flight to Albuquerque, New Mexico, I joined the rest of the passengers heading to U.S. Customs for processing. There were roughly over 300 foreign passengers in line, and my next flight was in less than an hour. Not knowing what to do if I missed my connecting flight, I anxiously waited for thirty minutes as the queue barely moved. The Washington State weather was different, and I felt my body getting colder. I had forgotten to grab a jacket from my checked luggage, so I shivered slightly. Everything around me looked different but exciting; the airport was well-organized and beautiful, and everyone seemed to move with a purpose. I felt a mix of excitement and exhaustion, aware that I needed to focus on the next steps.

With my connecting flight down to about half an hour away and the queue looking like it would take longer, I realized I might miss my flight and have to wait until the next day. I hesitated before leaving the line. I showed my boarding pass to the other student I previously met and he urged me to seek help. After some hesitation, I approached a kind-looking, motherly crew working there. Showing her my boarding pass, she immediately held my hand and led me to the front of the line, telling an official, "This boy needs to catch the next flight; he is a student, and he can't miss the flight." Her swift action and kindness saved the day, ensuring I could continue my journey.

I approached yet another familiar counter, this time for U.S. Customs, and handed over my travel documents to a gentleman in uniform who greeted me with a warm smile. His excitement upon seeing an international student was palpable, a rare and genuine enthusiasm that put me at ease. He asked why I had come to the United States, and I told him about my aspiration to receive the best education in the world, aiming to secure opportunities globally. He nodded with understanding, appreciating my ambition. After a brief but encouraging conversation, he stamped my passport with a sense of ceremony, as if marking the beginning of a significant chapter in my life. With a hearty handshake and a sincere wish for success, he sent me on my way, ready for the next leg of my journey to Durango, Colorado. This small interaction left me feeling welcomed and optimistic about the adventures and challenges that lay ahead.

The next stage was chaotic and clustered luggage claim, where I had to locate my checked bag and recheck it for my connecting flight. With hundreds of bags around and time running out, I frantically searched for about fifteen minutes. Just when I was about to give up, I saw my luggage coming through the conveyor. I immediately grabbed it and given the weight, it almost matched my size. Thankful for the luggage crew's instruction to leave it behind and proceed to the next gate, I sprinted to the next gate with less than ten minutes left. Anxiety about missing the flight gripped me as I navigated the huge airport, following signs and occasionally double-checking with staff to make sure I was headed in the right direction. If you had seen me, you would have thought I was running away from airport security, but I was not the only one; a few others were also running in the opposite direction, and I was convinced that I was doing the right thing.

Finally, I arrived at the gate, only to find it closed with a single crew member shutting the door. She asked if my last name was Mutai and, upon my confirmation, quickly walked me through the closed gate corridor, knocking on the plane's door, which had already shut. This was a clear sign that the customer service was willing to go above and beyond, a level of service not likely to be received at other airports. Amazingly, the door that was shut was opened, and I was welcomed aboard by a friendly air hostess who smiled warmly and walked me to my seat, gently placing my luggage in the compartment. I was the last passenger, and they must have waited a few extra minutes for me. My running skills had saved the day, and I couldn't help but feel a mix of relief and triumph as I settled into my seat.

At this point, the time zone had shifted, and I remember glancing at the clock next to the passenger beside me; it was around 6 p.m., late in the afternoon. Back home, it was the middle of the night, a time when I would typically be sleeping. The majority of the passengers on this flight were

Americans, with a few individuals of other races, including myself. I was tired and run down, but my excitement dulled any sense of hunger. The flight to Albuquerque, New Mexico, was about four hours long, and as soon as I sat down, I fell into a deep sleep, my dreams taking me right back home. I missed the takeoff and all the announcements that came with it. If there were any snacks and sodas served along the way, I must have missed them as well. I missed the pilot's landing instructions, something I had always looked forward to hearing.

The plane wheels descended with a noticeable hum, breaking the smooth monotony of the flight and waking me from my deep sleep. As they extended and locked into place, a subtle vibration reverberated through the cabin, growing stronger as the aircraft began its final approach. The sound of the wheels meeting the runway was a mixture of a muted thud and a gentle screech, signaling our descent above the city of Albuquerque, New Mexico.

The sudden shift from airborne tranquility to the tactile reality of landing jolted me awake, drawing my gaze to the window where the sprawling cityscape came into view, bathed in the warm hues of late evening light. It was dark outside, and the local time, as announced by the crew, was around 9 p.m. I had no cell phone to communicate with the rest of the world to let them know I had arrived and to be on the lookout for pick-up. Despite the absence of a cell phone, I remained confident that someone would be coming for me, based on the last email I had sent out a few days ago. The uncertainty of the moment was tempered by my faith in my prior arrangements, and I trusted that my arrival wouldn't go unnoticed.

As the plane taxied to the gate, the air hostess's voice came over the intercom, offering a last set of instructions. She reminded us, "If this is your final destination, please make your way to baggage claim upon exiting the aircraft to collect your checked-in bags." The tone was reassuring, yet I couldn't shake the uneasy feeling that my luggage might not have made it through the journey with me. Nonetheless, I mentally noted her advice, ready to navigate the next steps and hoping for the best as we prepared to exit.

As the passengers prepared to exit, I wasn't in a rush since I had no confirmation of pick-up, though I hoped someone was coming. Eventually, I exited the plane with my backpack, feeling energetic again. The journey had been filled with smiles, and I found myself waving and smiling at those around me. Clearing customs did not happen since this was my final destination. I proceeded to the luggage claim, with a nagging feeling that my checked luggage hadn't made it. After about half an hour, all the luggage had been collected by their owners, leaving a few unclaimed bags going round and round. A tall gentleman in uniform approached me and informed me that those were all the bags from our flight. He then kindly directed me to the luggage claim desk, and I thanked him for his assistance.

At the claim desk, another gentleman, who seemed to have been doing the job for over ten years, asked to check my passport. With a glance, he remarked that it must have been a very long journey, and I agreed. Out of curiosity, he asked where I was headed and if anyone was coming to pick me up. The conversation was smooth, though I had to adjust to his American accent, understanding that this was just the beginning of such interactions and I was up for the challenge. When I initially checked in my luggage, the tracker was stuck to the back of my passport, but due to my inexperience, I moved it to the inside cover. This complicated things for the gentleman as he kept searching for it, even looking through my backpack. Curious, I asked him what he was looking for and discreetly showed him the tracker inside the passport without revealing that I had moved it. From there, he proceeded to file a report for the missing luggage, using the address on my admission letter as the shipping address and adding my coach's phone number as the point of contact.

As soon as I was done, the gentleman asked if I needed help calling a taxi. I thanked him and assured him that everything was in order, and he then walked me to a waiting area. The area was empty, with everyone else heading towards what seemed like the exit. Despite the darkness, the place was beautiful, and I could see cars of various sizes stopping to pick up passengers. Most of them seemed to be family members, exchanging hugs and kisses as they reunited. The buildings looked different, and I began to admire the surroundings. After about an hour, I took out my notebook with about a hundred phone contacts, with the Kenyan coach's number at the top since he was my ride to Durango. I hesitated to stop passing passengers to borrow their cell phones, something I wasn't used to. Just as I was about to stand up and ask someone, I saw a mid-tall man and a brown lady approaching. They were both smiling, and the man's appearance perfectly matched the description of the stranger I had been speaking to over the phone. My ride to Durango, Colorado, had arrived.

CHAPTER 6

FIRST IMPRESSIONS AND NEW ADVENTURES

As the assistant coach, who I'll call Uncle, approached, his smile grew bigger, and the excitement on his face was unmistakable. He was genuinely happy to see me, and hearing him speak in Swahili for the second time since I left was thrilling. Despite the freezing weather, he wore shorts, sneakers, a t-shirt, and a backward ball cap, looking stunning and making me feel reassured that I had landed in the right place and was in good hands. The coach's companion, neither tall nor short, was cheerful to see that my journey had come to an end. She greeted me warmly, introduced herself, and was curious about my luggage. After a series of conversations and catching up about the flight, they walked me through the exit, and we headed towards the parking lot.

As we arrived at the parking lot, there was the ride: a brand-new, maroon Toyota Corolla. Before entering the vehicle, I walked around it as if conducting a mandatory inspection, complimenting how good it looked and how fresh it smelled. The Corolla's interior was equally impressive, boasting comfortable canvas seats that offered both durability and a refined texture. The seats were ergonomically designed, providing excellent support for long drives. The dashboard featured a high-resolution touchscreen display with intuitive controls for navigation, audio, and climate settings. The multifunction steering wheel, wrapped in soft leather, included controls for audio, phone, and cruise control, ensuring a seamless and hands-free driving experience.

As I settled down in the back seat, I smiled and began asking the coach numerous questions, which kept him and his wife laughing. Coming from a background where I was used to beat-up public transportation, often overcrowded and with comfort always coming last, this experience felt like pure luxury. The journey to Durango began with my uncle behind the wheel, marking the start of a new adventure.

After a few miles of discussing my flight experience, the car came to a complete stop at a gas station, which we referred to as a petrol station back home. It was dark, and there was nobody at the pump. Immediately, I reminded them that the petrol station was closed, and they laughed so hard that I thought I must have said something silly. I paid close attention and saw Uncle pumping what appeared to be petrol, and we took off again after his companion took over as the driver. I quietly asked the coach in Swahili if he had just stolen the gas, and he immediately translated my question to the driver, causing them both to burst into laughter. To cut the story short, he patiently explained how the self-service system worked, and it was unbelievable to me. That was the first lesson I learned in my new environment.

The driver skillfully navigated her way out of Albuquerque, seamlessly transitioning from local streets to a major freeway. She used the GPS with remarkable ease, her fingers deftly tapping the touchscreen to input our destination. The GPS's calm, clear voice provided turn-by-turn directions, and she followed them with confidence, making precise turns and lane changes as needed. Her familiarity with the city's layout and the technology at her fingertips left me in awe.

The route on the GPS screen displayed a series of colorful lines and arrows, guiding us through the maze of city roads and onto the freeway. I watched in amazement as the driver smoothly merged onto the busy highway, maintaining a steady speed and effortlessly blending into the flow of traffic. The entire process was fascinating to me, a stark contrast to the chaotic and often haphazard navigation I was used to back home. Her proficiency with the GPS and her composed driving underscored the advanced and organized nature of my new surroundings, making me feel both excited and reassured about the journey ahead.

The journey to Durango was about 215 miles by road, approximately 346 kilometers—a distance longer than any I had ever traveled. It was dark, and I could see little beyond the speeding vehicles beside us on the three-lane tarmacked road, perfectly illuminated by streetlights. Coach kept me engaged in conversation as I admired the driver's skills on the road. After about half an hour, the combination of comfort, the smooth road, and the beautiful South African music featuring *Sarafina* lulled me into a deep sleep, my thoughts drifting away.

I woke up as we arrived in Durango, Colorado, a little after 2 a.m. Exhausted but relieved that the journey was safe, I took in the town's beauty despite the darkness. Everything looked different, almost dreamlike. One notable difference was the weather; it was late August, and it was cold—a stark contrast I was sure I would never adjust to. The coach welcomed me to his house, my eyes adjusted to the dim lighting, and even the outlet sockets appeared different from what I was accustomed to. Attempting to relax, I removed my shoes and settled onto the couch. Despite the effort to make myself comfortable, the unfamiliar environment made it challenging to fully unwind. The coach then handed me a sleeping bag. I laughed, but he assured me it would work like magic.

Using a sleeping bag for the first time marked the beginning of a new adventure for me. As I unrolled the thick, insulated fabric and zipped myself in, I felt a mix of excitement and novelty. The cozy confines of the sleeping bag were unlike any bedding I had experienced before, wrapping me in warmth and comfort. The rustling sound of the material and the snug fit made me feel secure, almost as if I were being embraced by the promise of future adventures. Lying there, staring up at the unfamiliar ceiling of my new surroundings, I couldn't help but smile. This small yet significant moment symbolized the start of my journey, filled with new experiences and opportunities waiting to be explored.

Due to my exhaustion and lack of sufficient sleep, the night felt incredibly short. Around seven in the morning, a soft voice woke me, urging me to get ready for training camp. I immediately jumped out of my comfy bed, still tired but filled with excitement. After quickly washing my face, I followed the coach to his car. As we drove, he briefed me on the day's plan.

Seated in the front seat, I marveled at Durango's breathtaking landscape, a striking contrast of natural beauty and brisk weather, especially in the mountainous regions. The air was crisp and cool, a refreshing change from the summer heat I'd known. The towering Rocky Mountains, with their rugged peaks, enveloped the area, creating a dramatic and picturesque backdrop. These majestic mountains, often graced with patches of lingering snow even in late summer, added to the enchanting scenery. The beauty was real, and I felt a surge of excitement as I took it all in.

We soon arrived at the campsite, located in one of the most beautiful places up in the mountains. However, we did not drive there on the first day. Instead, we went to meet up with the team training on Country Road 150, about 15 miles from Fort Lewis College. I met the head coach, easily recognizable from his photograph on the website and the family picture he had sent me. His voice sounded exactly as it did when we talked on the phone, though his accent made it challenging to understand him, and vice versa. Nevertheless, I could tell he was pleased that I had arrived safely. I shook hands with a few teammates who were not running at that moment. One of them was a fellow Kenyan, who was particularly excited to meet another student embarking on the same journey. Although I couldn't remember all their names, they were cheerful and welcoming, thrilled to have an international team member join their ranks.

We then drove off to register at the college, the main reason I had come to the United States. As we drove up the hill to the college, I began recognizing buildings that looked exactly like the ones on the school website. Fort Lewis College, nestled in the scenic town of Durango, Colorado, offers a breathtaking campus surrounded by majestic mountain features and lush greenery. The serene environment is accentuated by deer grazing peacefully on the verdant lawns, creating a harmonious connection with nature. Unique architectural buildings dot the landscape, each with its distinct character, contributing to the college's charm. The Skyhawk mascot, symbolizing strength and aspiration, proudly represents the institution's spirit. For many students, attending Fort Lewis College feels like a dream coming unbelievably true, as they find themselves achieving their goals in this inspiring and beautiful setting.

Registration was a breeze, with everything already in the system. It was the best experience ever; the customer service was not only excellent but also a shock to me, as I had never experienced anything like it before. I wondered if it was because I was an international student, but the coach assured me that this level of service was the norm. Reflecting on home, I couldn't recall any college or university with such organization and customer service. Registration was completed in just a few minutes, and we then proceeded to check in at the housing. This process was also smooth because I had applied online, and a room was already assigned to me. I was handed a key, and we went to check out the room with the coach. It was a nice cubicle with two beds. My roommate, a friendly football player, was already checked in and playing video games. He greeted me warmly and offered to help if I needed anything or had any questions.

CHAPTER 7

CROSSING HURDLES

IF YOU'VE EVER FELT LIKE YOU WEREN'T GOOD ENOUGH FOR something you signed up for, you'll understand how I felt when the cross-country season started. I was introduced to the rest of the team, and they all seemed ready to compete. The cross-country camp, located at a scenic campsite just a few miles away from Fort Lewis College, was an immersive experience filled with unique and diverse meals.

My teammates were constantly conversing, eagerly discussing how the season would be successful, especially with the addition of an international team player. Although I could barely understand their conversations, my Kenyan brother was invaluable, always filling me in with the necessary information. At that time, he was neither short nor tall. He was a smart, good-looking individual who was always ahead of schedule. Known for his cheerful attitude, his instructions were clear and precise. He maintained a positive attitude, ensuring clarity and understanding within the team whenever something was not clear. His presence was instrumental in keeping everyone on track.

The cross-country season traditionally kicked off with a camp scheduled every fall, typically a week before the fall semester began. This camp was an ideal time to recruit new members to replace the graduating seniors. It provided a perfect opportunity for the entire team to come together, set goals for the upcoming season, and allow teammates to meet and get to know each other.

The Lodge was a two-story lodge located 30 miles north of Durango. Situated within and surrounded by the San Juan National Forest, it sits at an elevation of about 9,000 feet above sea level. The majestic mountains provide a spectacular view from the lodge, making it an ideal place to build endurance.

Each morning, a variety of breakfasts were offered, mostly composed of fruits, juice, and other nutritious fruit bars. We would gather around the huge table to eat and hydrate. I was surprised that the food never ran out, and the team always had plenty for short trips and snacks throughout the day. My go-to breakfast was a banana and sometimes bread, but with the help of my teammates, I discovered peanut butter and jelly sandwiches, which quickly became my staple food. It was different, and I embraced the change. Anyone who has traveled to a foreign country knows that after three or four days, your mouth starts itching to bite into something familiar.

Long runs in the morning were the main event, designed to build the endurance required for competing in 8KM and 10KM races. Despite the steep terrain, we trained hard, often finding the pack that suited our pace. Sometimes, towards the end of the camp, we were rewarded with a fun pool activity at Durango Hot Springs. Afterward, our head coach's family would invite us for dinner. The family was an absolute delight—warm, welcoming, and instantly making us feel at home. Their kindness and hospitality were truly remarkable, as they effortlessly made us feel like an integral part of their family. The kids were a joy to be around, with their contagious smiles and genuine enthusiasm. Meanwhile, the coach's wife's motherly warmth and open-heartedness created an atmosphere of comfort and belonging, ensuring that we felt loved and appreciated during our stay. It was clear that the bond within this family ran deep, and we were honored to be invited into their world. The team became like a family, and it became more than just training to compete for the season.

The head coach's preferred location for testing the fortitude of his runners was Missionary Ridge Road, situated on County Road 253. On that particular morning, he emphasized the importance of staying hydrated. Despite my inexperience with the terrain, I didn't fully grasp the magnitude of the challenge that lay ahead. My Kenyan brother advised me to eat some bananas, promising I'd be grateful later—a suggestion I'd soon come to appreciate.

As we traveled by bus, I was captivated by the scenic beauty of Durango, distracted by the sights and unfamiliar with the arduous task that awaited us. Upon arrival, I caught a glimpse of the inviting dirt road and decided to test it out with a brief run, only to be reminded that I should conserve my energy. It was at this location that I witnessed a bewildering scene—a golden retriever dutifully retrieving mail from a mailbox. My astonishment was met with amusement by the coach as I questioned the bewildering sight, wondering what other surprises this place had in store.

The instructions for the run were simple yet daunting: keep running as far as you can, and the bus will pick us up. An eclectic group of hard chargers—varying in height and build, yet uniformly dressed in athletic gear—assembled, and we were off. As we began our ascent up the seemingly endless, steep hill with an elevation of 9,480 feet, I found myself glancing at the watch of a nearby runner. Twelve minutes in, my lungs burned as if we had been running for an hour. Ahead of me, Egan and a few other shirtless runners maintained a steady conversation, seemingly unaffected by the grueling challenge.

As the arduous journey continued, I questioned my decision to be there, occasionally feeling it would have been better to stay where I was. But it was too late to back out; the local newspaper, Durango Herald, had already announced the arrival of Kenyan runners joining the team. After an hour of relentless effort, we finally reached what appeared to be the summit, having covered nearly seven miles. My sense of accomplishment and newfound confidence in my ability to contribute to the team surged.

As the bus arrived to pick up the remaining runners, the looks on the coaches' faces spoke volumes—I was a promising candidate and a worthwhile investment for the team.

Despite the other athlete's help, there were times I found myself alone when the rest of the team gathered for huddles, filling the gap of missing information and cultural nuances. Adjusting to the camp was challenging. Mornings were tough as I woke up yawning, frequently having flashbacks about home and constantly reassuring myself that I would be okay. Fortunately, my close friend was a great help. He explained everything I needed to know, guided me on where to be, and made sure I knew what time to get up the next day, providing a comforting sense of familiarity and support in an otherwise difficult transition.

The next day, I sat down with the head coach to get to know him and answered questions about my home, training schedule, and intentions for the team throughout the year. I was honest to the best of my ability, sharing my strengths and weaknesses and what I needed help with, especially once school started. I reminded him that I hadn't been in a classroom environment for some time now, which was my main reason for coming to the United States. I found it easier not to give myself credit because I wasn't sure how I measured up to the rest of the group. They appeared to be in better shape, so I confessed that I was not in peak condition but promised to work extra hard to catch up. Despite the challenges ahead, I felt excited and motivated by the opportunities that lay before me.

The camp was scheduled for a week to prepare for the upcoming cross-country season. It was fun, but I was always exhausted at the end of the day due to the long runs and stretches. Adjusting to the elevation of over 6,500 feet above sea level was challenging, and it was consistently cold throughout the day. My luggage hadn't arrived, leaving me short on clothes, so my assistant coach kindly lent me some of his T-shirts and oversized shorts, which worked well for me. I had never run for more than an hour—my longest runs were 40-55 minutes—but my teammates ran for at least an hour with ease. I kept up, guided by my colleague who was in his second year and knew how to maintain the pace without overexerting. I quickly adapted and developed a deeper love for running. Although I wasn't familiar with proper stretching techniques for running, I learned them effortlessly.

I admired the beauty of the Colorado mountains, and every morning, despite the cold, I would go outside to gaze at them. There was a bit of snow on top, which I confirmed after asking, as I had always wanted to see snow. My friends informed me that snow time was just around the corner, so I needed to start preparing. Unlike the perfect weather back home, which warmed up during the day, the cold in Colorado persisted throughout, even when the sun was out. I struggled with the food, often feeling hungry as it was light and snack-based. Nevertheless, I blended in and tried to eat what everyone else was eating. This experience marked the first time I truly began to be independent, making my own decisions and adapting to a new environment.

As days went by, I began to get along well with my teammates. Though I was still new, I could sense they enjoyed my company, inviting me to play games, hang out, and talk about home and what to look forward to. Most of them were a few years younger than me and often couldn't believe my age due to my size. The team quickly turned into a family. Several figures played positive roles in my journey. One of the teammates, smart and kind, once pointed out the type of food I might like, and her suggestions were spot on.

The team consisted of cheerful and goal-oriented teammates, always excited to keep up with the rest. Among them was an energetic runner with long hair, always ready to race, and a bald Army veteran eager to finish first. Another teammate was a smart, long-distance runner, capable of running for hours. Many teammates regularly checked on my progress, including a talkative, intelligent individual always ready to compete, a kind-hearted and caring runner who frequently looked out for me, and a short guy with a thick American accent and thick hair, who was a dreamer and always on top of his game.

Camping came to an end, and it was time to return to college for orientation and the start of classes. Fort Lewis College, a National Collegiate Athletic Association Division II school nestled in the breathtaking mountains of Durango, Colorado, had a vibrant excitement about orientation. The campus, with its stunning views and serene environment, felt like a perfect blend of natural beauty and academic promise. As I stepped into the bustling crowd of new students, a mix of excitement and nervousness washed over me. It was exhilarating to meet fellow students from diverse backgrounds, each with unique stories and dreams. The orientation sessions were filled with icebreakers, campus tours, and informative talks, all designed to help us transition smoothly into college life.

The transition to Fort Lewis College was a flurry of new experiences and opportunities. The internet and availability of computers all over campus 24/7, fast and reliable, was shocking and exciting. I fell in love with the campus and the people. Carrying a student identification card with my photograph on it, an upgrade from the laminated one from high school, felt like a significant milestone. With the help of my friend, a sophomore at the time, and alongside two other Kenyan student-athletes, the transition was smooth. Questions from other students about my journey and transition were common, and everyone was willing to help if I needed anything. It was different but wonderful to talk about where I came from and why I chose Fort Lewis College among other colleges in the United States.

I started feeling awesome and important again, and all the negativity and low self-esteem I had began to fade away. My skin started flaking off as I was no longer doing hard labor on the farm. The food was different too—milk was plentiful, and I could eat bread and drink soda whenever I wanted. I enjoyed every bit of the opportunity. I started feeling like a student again, carrying a backpack and reading books to blend in with the other students around campus became my hobby.

The college community also had a family host program that turned out to be helpful. I did not know what the program was all about, but I accepted the invitation before college. It was one of those checkboxes you have to fill in to complete an application, hoping it would be helpful someday. After all, it was the only thing I could do at that moment without even asking around what it was. I was a big boy, and I just thought maybe I could use some company but still was not sure why. I was open to anything. I started exchanging emails with the host parents, who by then I didn't know who they were. I was accustomed to exchanging emails with the coach for a long time, so I figured, why not, since I was already in the U.S. I started knowing about them through emails and sometimes phone calls.

The host family was an extraordinary family who played a pivotal role in my college transition. Their warmth, kindness, and generosity created a nurturing environment that felt like a home away from home. From the moment I arrived, their genuine hospitality and welcoming nature made me feel like part of the family. The thoughtfully prepared meals engaging stories and guidance provided me with a sense of comfort and support during a time of significant change. Their kindness extended beyond their home as they helped me navigate the new campus and community, easing my transition and setting me on a path toward success in college. The host family became more than just a temporary shelter; they were a beacon of inspiration, support, and friendship that shaped my college experience in the most meaningful way.

As I adjusted to my new college life, I vividly recall the day I spotted my host dad rolling into the parking lot with a 7-speed bicycle, his face beaming with excitement. Knowing that this generous gift would help me navigate the vast campus more efficiently, I was filled with gratitude and a growing affection for my host family. Their unwavering love and support not only contributed to my academic success but also instilled in me a profound appreciation for the few selfless individuals in the world who genuinely care for others.

My host mom's motherly instincts shone brightly when she shopped for my winter clothes, an experience that transported me back to the tender moments of my childhood. Her willingness to invest a significant amount of money in my comfort and well-being was a level of thoughtfulness and generosity I had never before encountered. This extraordinary treatment further solidified the deep connection I felt with my host parents, a connection that shaped my college journey and left a lasting impression on my heart. Their presence filled the void left by my parents, who were thousands of miles away on foreign soil.

An extraordinary way for my host parents to connect with us on occasion was by arranging dinners in downtown Durango. These gatherings were truly memorable, as they provided an opportunity to learn about fine dining and refine my etiquette. Observing my host mother ordering food in a sophisticated manner, which even included appetizers—something I had previously perceived as the main dish—was an eye-opening experience that often left me feeling full before the meal even arrived.

Every dinner gathering was inspiring, but one occasion, in particular, stood out. We found ourselves seated among highly educated professionals, a rare opportunity to engage with individuals of such caliber. One notable guest was a neurosurgeon, an encounter that forever shifted my perspective on the value of taking full advantage of the education system. Never before had I met a neurosurgeon, let alone exchanged a handshake and heard firsthand the specialized terminology that would likely be absent from my home dictionary. This dinner served as a powerful reminder that no dream is too ambitious to achieve, as long as one is determined to pursue it wholeheartedly.

A missionary family, a couple with a history of mission work in various parts of Kenya, discovered that Kenyan students were attending the college. They took the initiative to reach out and arrange a meet and greet to connect with these students. They were both an abundance of knowledge and wisdom, they all became a supportive parental figure who played a crucial role in helping me adapt to our new environment.

CHAPTER 8

NAVIGATING A NEW ACADEMIC LANDSCAPE

RETURNING TO CLASS FOR THE FIRST TIME AFTER HIGH school back home was a significant milestone. I met with an international student advisor who provided counseling on the expectations for international students and assisted me with class registration. Fortunately, everything went as planned, and I was enrolled in general courses that all seemed new and exciting. As a student-athlete, I was required to take a minimum of 12 credit units to be eligible to compete on the team, so I navigated this unfamiliar system with determination. I received a detailed timetable that outlined when and where my classes were held, ensuring I was prepared and ready to embrace this new academic journey.

The student advisor, a patient professional walked me through all the courses, clearly outlining the requirements and expectations. His detailed explanations and genuine concern for my success turned my efforts into a collaborative endeavor. Listening to his guidance and observing his dedication made me feel supported and motivated. His wealth of experience provided me with a clear direction, ensuring I knew exactly what I needed to do and focus on to succeed.

Classes began on the scheduled date, and everything proceeded smoothly, with all the students showing up as planned. It didn't feel like the first day because everything was so orderly and efficient, with no time wasted. I arrived in class five minutes early, yet I was still among the last to enter; everyone else was already seated and ready to start. The first day mostly involved introductory discussions about the syllabus and the semester's requirements. Having just arrived from Kenya, I found myself in a classroom where all the teachers were Americans and spoke a foreign language.

Although I was proficient in English, I struggled to understand the professors due to their accents and rapid speech. It often felt like I was listening to a radio broadcast but with the speakers standing right in front of me. I frequently found myself thinking about home, only snapping back to reality when the class ended, prompting me to head to my next session. I missed the nuances and humor of the class; whenever the professor made a joke and everyone laughed, I would just smile, clueless about what was funny.

Stepping into the classroom for the first time as an international student, I felt an overwhelming sense of being lost. The unfamiliar environment, the fast-paced conversations in a language that wasn't my usual way or speaking or Swahili, and the new academic system all contributed to my confusion. My thoughts frequently drifted back home, intensifying my homesickness and longing for the familiarity and comfort of my own country. Despite this, I knew I had to push through these feelings. I reminded myself that knowledge had to be injected into my brain, and this was the first step towards achieving my dreams. The challenge of adapting to this new academic life was daunting, but the determination to succeed and make the most of this opportunity kept me focused, even amidst the waves of homesickness and disorientation.

Adjusting to the new culture added another layer of complexity, as I struggled to keep up with the pace and nuances of college life. In College Algebra, I scored a disappointing 70% on my first exam, while my peers scored over 90%, which was a wake-up call for me. This motivated me to put in extra effort, seeking help from tutors and attending additional study sessions. Gradually, my hard work paid off, and by the end of the semester, I had significantly improved my grades, gaining confidence and a better understanding of the academic expectations at Fort Lewis College.

During the first week, I missed some assignments. I recall one instance when my math professor asked if I had completed the homework. I confessed that I was unaware of any assignment, and he advised me to stay after class to address any questions.

The professor was excellent and always directed me to the student tutors available throughout the week. By the second week, I had adjusted and stopped missing assignments. All the instructors were friendly and willing to help in any way possible. I borrowed the required textbooks and a calculator for my first semester, which would have otherwise cost me over a hundred dollars. With blankets and personal hygiene items having already consumed half of my budget, I was left with only thirty dollars. Consequently, I had to be very careful with my spending.

The cross-country schedule soon kicked in, requiring me to muster on the field after classes for practice. This was a significant change, as I found myself juggling the demands of homework with long runs alongside my team. It was challenging, and at times I questioned why I was doing it. However, I kept reminding myself that it was for the betterment of my future and my family. Both coaches were incredibly supportive, constantly checking in on my academic progress. I was honest with them and made sure to stay on top of my classwork.

By the third week, I had adapted to the schedule, becoming more independent and familiar with the campus and my routine. I even found extra time to browse the internet, read news from home, chat with friends on Facebook, and post beautiful photos of my new surroundings. Everyone back home loved it, and I began to see my journey as a dream and a blessing realized after many years. Additionally, I kept in touch with my younger brother, who was attending college in Wyoming. We spoke every other day, and his advice provided me with the answers I needed to navigate my new life.

The fall semester is cross-country season for colleges, and after classes, whether tired or not, the coach was always waiting on the field at 3:45 p.m. from Monday through Friday to get us in shape for upcoming meets with colleges in the region. It was a new schedule I had to adjust to, balancing the demands of academics with rigorous training sessions. This routine required a great deal of discipline and perseverance, but it was essential for preparing us for the competitive season ahead. Both my academic and athletic life kept me busy.

I enjoyed most of the classes, but there were a few I struggled to understand, particularly American history. This subject had always been difficult for me, and I had no prior knowledge of U.S. history. The history professor, who had likely been teaching for years and was full of knowledge, knew the material so well that he never used PowerPoints, which I typically relied on. Instead, he dictated notes, leaving me bored. Frustrated, I visited his office one day to ask for help. He handed me an about 500-page history book, explaining that our lessons were based on it. Although I thanked him for his effort, I felt overwhelmed and clueless as I attempted to read the book. It was incredibly challenging, and I felt completely out of my depth.

Taking an English Literature course was a daunting experience, as we were required to read a lengthy novel in just two weeks—something I was not used to. Back in high school, we studied literature novels too, but we typically had the entire school year in senior classes to read and analyze them, giving us ample time to revisit and thoroughly understand the material. The accelerated pace of this college course felt overwhelming, and I found myself struggling to keep up with the rapid reading schedule. The pressure to digest and interpret such a vast amount of content in a short period was challenging, and I had to quickly adapt to this new academic intensity.

Before the last day to drop deadline, I immediately sought help from the student advisor. I visited his office to see if he could help me change classes. He was very helpful, and I successfully dropped English literature and history, replacing them with international business and sociology. After making this change, everything began to fall into place. I was able to catch up and understand what was being taught. My new international business professor assured me that the class was manageable. She encouraged me to read ahead, ask questions, and seek her help whenever needed. The class was small, making it easier to engage, and I made a friend, who also assisted me with questions. We hung out in the lounge before class and sometimes discussed the material before tests, which greatly helped my understanding and adjustment.

Even though I was surrounded by many people and friends, it wasn't the same as being at home because everyone had different ways of spending their free time. My roommate was always playing video games, an interest I did not share, while I spent my time browsing and watching local YouTube music videos from famous musicians in Kenya and Tanzania. Despite these differences, I kept myself busy and developed a routine. I utilized my time well and eventually found a part-time job, which was necessary to pay for my health insurance required by the NCAA for athletic participation. As an international student, the cost was $90 per month. I didn't have the money for the first month, so my brother covered it for me. However, with the second month approaching, I didn't want to overburden him since he was also attending school and working a part-time job.

My social life on campus flourished as I connected with fellow students who shared common interests, creating a vibrant network of friends. Among the many individuals I met, a cheerful cafeteria supervisor stood out. He often engaged me in conversations about lions, giraffes, and safaris, eager to learn about my background. One day, I seized an opportunity and asked him about part-time job prospects. Without hesitation, he introduced me to his boss, who inquired about my motivations.

I shared my desire to cover insurance and personal expenses, prompting her to promptly draft an employment letter and after a series of paper work, I began my first shift the next week. Although my schedule became increasingly packed with lectures during the day, athletic practice after classes, and evening work hours, I persevered. Managing to work up to three-four hours a day in four days.

As I entered my second month, my hard work began to bear fruit. I was able to cover my expenses and made a significant purchase—a used Toshiba laptop from eBay that felt like new. This acquisition proved transformative, enabling me to complete assignments from the comfort of my hostel in the early morning and late-night hours. I could also stay connected with friends without relying on the computer lab. I continued to build my newfound financial stability by buying a cell phone, ensuring I remained connected with loved ones. Regularly sharing updates about my evolving life, I deepened the bond with my family, despite the distance between us. We exchanged prayers for protection and guidance until we could reunite, with the timing uncertain but our faith unwavering. I consistently sought God's wisdom in making better choices and maintaining good health throughout my journey.

CHAPTER 9

FROM PASSION TO PROFESSION

Back in high school, my last cross-country experience was alongside more skilled runners, and our runs would typically span thirty to forty minutes. Although I wasn't the best at it, the joy I derived from running was undeniable. Never had I imagined that I could transform my passion into a career; I had only heard of such stories where people made a living from running, but it seemed far-fetched to consider myself among them. Even my close friends would jokingly tease me about my slender frame, asserting that my thin legs were suited for running, not farming and that I should consider running professionally. At the time, I dismissed these compliments as mere banter. However, as I secured admission to college through athletics, the fantasies I once entertained back home began materializing into reality. I became determined to snatch the opportunity, conquer the challenges ahead, and create a legacy that would leave an indelible mark on history.

When I embarked on my journey at Fort Lewis College, one of the esteemed NCAA Division II colleges, with a projected graduation date in April 2013. Never once did doubt cloud my mind; instead, I channeled my energy into being present and focused, ensuring that I was always in the right place at the right time, doing the right thing. As an international student, I bore the responsibility of representing not only myself but also my country and my fellow Kenyans. Failure was not an option, and I refused to let myself become an example of academic struggles or a lagging cross-country runner after being given such a remarkable opportunity. Hailing from Kenya, I was determined to rise above expectations and prove my mettle. Deep down, I knew success was within reach; all I had to do was wait for the perfect moment to unfold.

Driven by an unwavering determination to avoid any negative outcomes, I diligently applied myself to uphold the reputation of my homeland and to validate the faith that my head coach had placed in me. I wanted him to feel a sense of pride in his decision to bring me to this college. With an unwavering focus on success, failure never entered my mind as a possibility. To achieve my goals, I dedicated additional hours to studying independently, seeking support from the learning resource center for subjects that required extra attention.

The college was well-equipped with resources, making it a stark contrast to my previous educational experiences. I knew that it would take a completely careless person to fail a class in this environment. The solutions to my challenges were within reach; all I had to do was seek them out to excel. I was well aware that success was easily attainable as long as I maintained my work ethic and made the right choices. Being alone and independent, without my older siblings to guide me, I understood that my destiny rested solely in my hands. Both success and failure were within my grasp, and I knew I had to make wise decisions to ensure a prosperous future.

Running was an activity that brought me immense joy. Our routes led us along the sides of roads and through trails in the woods, where the weather was consistently pleasant, albeit slightly chilly even when the sun shone. During these runs, I discovered numerous new experiences. Hikers, bikers, and even vehicles would yield to our path, with some automobiles coming to a complete stop until we had all passed. This was a remarkable contrast to my experiences back home, where encountering a vehicle often meant running for one's life. The consideration and courtesy I encountered here only added to my love for running. While many of the boys preferred to run shirtless, I never dared to try it, as I was perpetually cold and unwilling to risk feeling even colder.

It soon became clear to me that athletics, particularly cross-country, held great importance and recognition throughout the United States. The athletics department at my college was expansive and under the supervision of dedicated coaches. Our daily practice sessions were designed to prepare us for intense competitions against other colleges in the region. While some friendly events allowed us to gauge our strengths, the final three events—conference, regional, and championship—were the ultimate tests of our abilities. In the lead-up to these significant competitions, we trained rigorously from Monday to Saturday, with our coach identifying areas for improvement among team members.

Despite the reassurance from my Kenyan brother, I couldn't help but feel nervous before each run. My anxiety stemmed from the seemingly superior physical condition of my taller and healthier teammates. However, I refused to let my apprehension consume me.

One of the greatest challenges I faced was acclimating to the high elevation and frigid winds that often left my lips dry and skin flaky. Following each run, my body experienced fatigue and muscle cramps, but my observant nature and willingness to seek advice allowed me to learn effective stretching techniques from my teammates. Over time, I acquired valuable knowledge about running, and everything began to fall into place.

To assemble the strongest team possible, the coach organized trials to select the top five runners to represent the college, while the remaining athletes served as replacements in case of injuries or unforeseen circumstances. As an international student hailing from Kenya, I was determined not to be relegated to the role of a mere replacement, as it could raise questions, bring embarrassment, and potentially put my contract at risk. My nerves were on edge during the initial trial, but as the run progressed alongside my teammates, I found myself gaining confidence and feeling more at ease.

Despite the difficulty in breathing and the bouts of nausea that followed our one-mile repeats, the coach's observant gaze and words of encouragement fueled my motivation to continue pushing myself. With additional guidance and support from my Kenyan coach and friend, I cultivated both endurance and speed, developing a deeper appreciation for running in the process.

To further enhance our performance, we took it upon ourselves to engage in extra training sessions during the early hours of Sunday mornings and on other days throughout the week. These additional miles and endurance workouts proved to be a turning point in our progress, making a noticeable impact on our performance. Our coach, however, expressed concerns about our strength during practice and occasionally requested that we slow down, allowing the rest of the team to keep up with our pace.

A seasoned runner and a Kenyan brother became my dedicated training companion, pushing me to surpass my perceived boundaries. Our daily rendezvous at Snyder Halls, his place of residence, commenced at the break of dawn—6 a.m. sharp. With an appearance akin to the iconic athlete Kipchoge, he exuded an undeniable air of fitness and determination. As he engaged his stopwatch, we launched into our intensive workouts, striving for excellence with each passing moment.

After fifteen minutes, we reached a detour along East College Drive, and as I struggled to catch my breath due to the 7,000-foot elevation, this guy halted our run. Deep down, I feared he was contemplating something even more intense. My suspicions were confirmed as he sprinted up a steep, daunting hill, nearly 120 meters high—a slope so challenging that not even a 7-speed bicycle could conquer it. Before I could question him, he dashed off, leaving me no choice but to follow. We alternated hill sprints, pushing ourselves up and jogging back down.

Our uphill battle continued with eight to ten repetitions, and for the first time, I found myself questioning how I ended up in this situation. Nevertheless, quitting was never an option. Over time, we grew accustomed to the demanding routine, and we knew we were in peak shape if we could complete all ten cycles without the urge to throw up.

Among the many memorable experiences, the assistant coach's willingness to instruct us during morning training sessions left a lasting impression. His favored technique, which he considered his secret weapon, revolved around speed work on the wide-shouldered East College Drive—another steep and less-trafficked road intended for bikers.

Using the electric poles lining the road, approximately 40 meters apart, the assistant coach instructed us to sprint from one pole to the next, utilizing the distance between the poles for recovery through a light jog rather than walking. This intense cycle, repeated six times following a twenty-minute warm-up jog, left us questioning the purpose behind such a demanding regimen. On those days, the prospect of canceled classes seemed like a godsend, offering much-needed time to recover from the arduous training session.

Another memorable moment was a Sunday morning long run along Highway 550 in Durango. It looked like that day my Kenyan brother decided he was bored and volunteered to take me on a spin. We met in a parking lot where he normally parked his car and drove off a few miles down the road, where he parked his car outside the coaches' residence.

By that time, we were fully in shape, ready to dare anyone to race. That particular morning, we raced, taking turns on the lead until we got the attention of a highway patrol who happened to be cruising by. The look on his face was awe, and his concern that we were on fire was accurate. His face registered a mix of awe and concern as if he believed we were figuratively on fire due to our intense speed and determination.

The training and coaching were paying off; by mid-season, our remarkable speed was difficult for anyone who wasn't in peak shape to keep up with. One particular Saturday morning, we trained at Durango High School, with a warm-up followed by four-to-five-mile repeats. Knowing that the intensity might lead to someone throwing up, we skipped breakfast that day. The first mile was relatively easy, and we clocked in at 5 minutes and 30 seconds. The second mile was faster by about fifteen seconds. As we raced for the final mile, we managed an incredible 4 minutes and 20 seconds—a feat that left the coach amazed and questioning what had just occurred.

Our intense speed and competitive spirit that day caused a couple of our teammates to vomit, but it was all in good fun. For the first time, the coach felt compelled to remind us that it was only a training session and encouraged us to take it easier in the future to prevent injuries and save the rest for regionals.

CHAPTER 10

HOME MEET

A home meet in cross country serves as a significant event for the Fort Lewis College cross country team, providing an opportunity to showcase their talents on familiar terrain. It allows the team to compete in a supportive environment where friends, family, and the college community, including our beloved Skyhawks mascot, can come together to cheer them on. This event fosters school spirit and reinforces the athletes' sense of belonging and pride in their institution. For the team, it means running with the advantage of knowing the course's nuances, boosting their confidence and performance. Additionally, a home meet strengthens team unity and team spirit, as they work together to defend their home turf and achieve collective success. I was happy to be among this incredible team, sharing in the excitement and pride of representing Fort Lewis College.

Nestled atop a photogenic mesa overlooking the charming town of Durango, Colorado, the Hillcrest Golf Course served as the designated site for our homecoming cross-country events. Just a stone's throw away from the Fort Lewis College campus, this remarkable location offers an unparalleled combination of convenience and natural beauty that truly sets it apart within the Four Corners region.

Surrounded by the majestic Southern Colorado Rockies, Hillcrest Golf Course encapsulates the essence of Durango's breathtaking landscape. With its tranquil atmosphere and stunning views, it presents an ideal opportunity for athletes and spectators alike to fully immerse themselves in the region's splendor while partaking in the excitement of the cross-country event.

My inaugural race on this course marked the start of my cross-country adventure. After training diligently for a few weeks, I was eager to put my running skills to the test. Clad in the coach's carefully selected racing attire, I enthusiastically prepared for the competition. My feet were snugly wrapped in flat racing shoes, providing the perfect balance of comfort and agility. Donning the Skyhawk's signature blue, I proudly wore the team's colors in a sleek, lightweight racing singlet that not only showcased my allegiance but also allowed for optimal mobility. Completing the ensemble, I slipped into my favorite pair of flying shorts, designed to maximize both speed and performance.

Adding a touch of professional flair, my chest bore a race chip timer, the same technology used in prestigious events like the Olympics. This technological marvel imbued the race with an aura of excitement and legitimacy, making me feel as though I was part of something significant. As I glanced at the chip timer, anticipation surged through my veins, and I knew I was ready to take on the challenges that awaited me on the cross-country course. It was during this race that I discovered the importance of pacing myself – unless you possess both endurance and speed, you're essentially just setting the pace for others to overtake you at the finish line.

I found myself competing against seasoned runners, including sophomores and seniors, who were well-versed in navigating the challenging slopes of the 8KM course. As the race commenced, we took off with enthusiasm and determination, ready to conquer the distance ahead. Feeling confident, I gave it my all, only to realize later that we had to conquer the hilly side of the course not once, not twice, but three times! This unexpected challenge served as a harsh reminder of the course's unforgiving terrain and tested the limits of my endurance.

Through this grueling 8 km race, I learned a valuable lesson in humility. My overconfidence was humbled by the course's unrelenting hills, teaching me that even with the best intentions and fervor, sometimes we find ourselves biting off more than we can chew – or, in my case, running up more hills than I could handle. The experience proved that understanding the intricacies of the course, maintaining a measured pace, and respecting the challenges ahead were crucial elements in successfully traversing the demanding landscape of a cross-country race.

Securing third place with an impressive time, just behind my teammates, I was filled with a sense of accomplishment. As fate would have it, another teammate had opted out of this race to conserve energy for more significant events. This stroke of luck propelled me into the spotlight, granting me the opportunity to participate in upcoming trials.

Reflecting on my performance, I reveled in the exhilaration of seeing my official time and the realization that I possessed untapped potential. This newfound awareness fueled my determination to push my limits in future races, understanding that I was capable of more while still preserving my ability to fight another day. Ultimately, the experience proved to be both exhilarating and enlightening, revealing a strength within myself that I had yet to fully explore.

In addition to participating in my race, I had the opportunity to spectate and cheer on the female athletes as they tackled a challenging 5KM course. Observing from the sidelines offered a unique perspective, and the race appeared deceptively easy compared to the firsthand experience of running it myself. As I enthusiastically cheered the runners on, urging them to push harder and give their best effort, I gained a newfound appreciation for the power of encouragement from spectators.

This experience allowed me to empathize with those who had cheered me on during my race, realizing the significant impact that supportive words and cheers could have on a competitor's determination and drive. By being a part of the spirited crowd, I witnessed firsthand how our collective energy and motivation could inspire and propel the athletes to dig deep and persevere through the challenging course. The connection between runner and spectator became evident, highlighting the importance of the shared enthusiasm that truly embodies the spirit of a cross-country event.

The unity forged among participants and spectators during the race was a testament to the strong social aspect of the event. Athletes and supporters from the Durango community united in their shared appreciation for the competitive spirit, transcending their roles as competitors and fans. A strong sense of unity permeated the gathering, with many attendees sporting Skyhawk apparel—a clear indication of their deep connection and devotion to the team that went beyond mere admiration. The race served as a powerful catalyst, bringing together individuals from all walks of life and reinforcing the bonds that make the Durango community truly special.

This collective enthusiasm showcased the Durango community's strong bond, emphasizing the importance of cross-country in bringing people together. More than just fans, these individuals embodied the essence of a tight-knit cross-country family, offering encouragement and support as they united in their shared love for the sport and their desire to uplift the athletes. Their presence served as a heartwarming reminder of the powerful impact that community involvement can have on fostering a sense of belonging and shared purpose.

Throughout my four-year college journey, I had the opportunity to partake in two additional home meets. One of these events saw me emerge victorious, claiming a well-deserved win. However, in another particular race, it was another seasoned Kenyan runner who dominated the field. With his extensive experience and unwavering determination, he proved himself a formidable opponent, leaving no doubt that he was serious about his craft when he donned his running gear.

CHAPTER 11

TRIUMPHS AND TRIALS

ALL OF OUR COMPETITIONS WERE HOSTED BY VARIOUS universities within the region. My first meet took place at Adams State University, with the course set on a golf course field at an elevation of around 7,000 feet above sea level. As a newcomer, the high altitude made the race particularly challenging, but the thought of quitting never crossed my mind.

Throughout the race, I grappled with my breathing and underestimated the significance of staying adequately hydrated. Despite these challenges, I persevered and completed the 8KM race with a time of 27 minutes and some seconds—a feat that exceeded the head coach's expectations, considering the high elevation. This milestone was an encouraging sign that I was steadily advancing towards my goals and adapting to the demanding environment.

In my sophomore year, I had the opportunity to run another race on the same challenging course. This time, I achieved a significant milestone by finishing in the top ten. This accomplishment was not just a testament to my hard work but also to the unwavering support and rigorous training provided by my teammates. Their encouragement and dedication played a crucial role in my success, pushing me to strive for excellence every step of the way. After crossing the finish line, the sense of achievement I felt was immeasurable, and I knew I couldn't have done it alone. We celebrated this victory together, each teammate sharing in the joy and pride of the moment. They had become more than just a team; they were my support system, my motivators, and my friends. Their belief in my abilities fueled my determination and resilience, making this victory a shared triumph.

The days flew by, and in the blink of an eye, I found myself growing more knowledgeable, developing positive habits, and becoming increasingly independent. This newfound independence allowed me to make swift and correct decisions, helping me steer clear of trouble.

My academic performance was good, as I never failed a class and witnessed my grades steadily improve with each passing semester. Maintaining a solid GPA bolstered my confidence that I was heading in the right direction. Staying diligent with homework assignments was crucial, as they comprised a substantial portion of my final grade. Whenever extra credit opportunities presented themselves in certain classes, I eagerly seized them.

For more challenging classes, I attended remedial sessions at the learning center, which greatly enhanced my understanding of the material and made classes feel more manageable. With these support systems in place, I was convinced that graduation was well within reach.

While my running abilities improved and I became one of the top performers, surpassing the coach's expectations, I encountered various challenges along the way. Leg injuries were particularly painful, forcing me to miss important events and sometimes attempt to run despite the pain, ultimately causing more harm. Thankfully, the coach was understanding and ensured I received treatment from athletic trainers. It took me some time to comprehend the reasons behind my frequent muscle injuries, which seemed inexplicable considering running was my primary activity.

The most severe injury I suffered was a stress fracture, which occurred mid-semester when the team relied on me the most. Despite seeking treatment from athletic trainers, I found no relief. With the regional competition fast approaching, I was determined to participate as one of the top five runners. The race took place in Nebraska during the frigid winter months, with temperatures plummeting to an unbearable -25 degrees Fahrenheit—a level of cold I had never experienced before.

Upon arriving at the golf course field, we discovered that the grass was completely frozen. In light of the extreme conditions, officials directed us to warm up inside the gym to prevent potential injuries.

The race was planned for noon, with the hope that the temperature would rise; unfortunately, it remained bitterly cold. As we stood at the starting line, donning our racing attire, it felt as if we were being burned by the freezing air. The intense cold not only made breathing a struggle, but it also numbed my legs and hands to the point where I couldn't even feel the pain in my injured left leg until after the race was over.

Despite the excruciating conditions, I managed to finish the race, though I was limping by the end due to the extreme pain. It felt as if my leg was broken, but I pushed through and accomplished my mission. Despite my perseverance, our team did not qualify for the championship, as other teams outperformed us.

Participating in cross-country was an incredibly enjoyable experience for me. Apart from the races, I had the opportunity to travel to numerous states for invitational meets, which was always exciting. Traveling on the college bus allowed us to explore various destinations, with Oklahoma being the furthest. One place I especially loved to boast about was Riverside, California, as it proved challenging to describe its beauty to my siblings back home.

During our journeys, we departed from college early in the morning. While the drives were lengthy and tiring for some, I found them exhilarating. We made frequent stops along the way for bathroom breaks, meals, snacks, and even impromptu running sessions. Equipped with a camera, I captured every moment of our trips, documenting the breathtaking scenery along the interstate, while my fellow teammates didn't share the same enthusiasm for photography.

As we approached Riverside, I noticed the roads widening, and I marveled at the advanced technology and the skilled drivers navigating their way to their destinations with ease. I felt an overwhelming sense of admiration for everything around me, ensuring that I preserved every memory with photographs.

Upon arriving at our destination, I immediately noticed a shift in temperature—it was warmer and more humid, which I found quite pleasant. I observed that the clock on my phone had changed, but it still displayed Mountain Time, the local time zone we used in Colorado. When I inquired about the time difference, I learned it was due to a state law passed to enable workers to have longer working days during daylight hours rather than nights.

Throughout the cross-country event, it became evident that everyone was deeply invested and engaged in the competition. Even the spectators who had traveled long distances were enthusiastic in their support. It was clear that sports were highly valued and respected in the United States. The families of our teammates had come from far away, bringing snacks, water, and sports drinks for the team members and documenting the event with pictures.

Another memorable race was an 8KM event hosted by the University of Colorado in Boulder. This race was particularly notable not just for its challenging course but also for its intense level of competition. Any athlete who has run this particular course can attest to its grueling nature. The course features beat-up grass, reminiscent of a once-thriving farm, and includes a steep hill approximately 150 meters long. We had to tackle this hill three times throughout the race, each ascent leaving our knees weak and our spirits tested. The terrain demanded every ounce of strength and endurance we possessed, pushing us beyond our perceived limits. The relentless ups and downs, combined with the uneven, rough patches of the course, tested not only our physical stamina but also our mental resilience.

Despite these challenges, the race served as a powerful catalyst for our team's growth. It bonded us through shared struggle and determination, as each of us fought to maintain our pace and support one another through the toughest stretches. The collective effort and perseverance required to navigate this demanding course brought out the best in us, turning the intense competition into an unforgettable experience. The togetherness and mutual encouragement within the team were evident, as we pushed ourselves and each other to finish strong. This race, with its unique blend of difficulty and solidarity, remains etched in my memory as a defining moment of our athletic journey, highlighting the resilience and unity that made our team exceptional.

Through my college running career, I accomplished a great deal, learning more about the sport and forming close friendships along the way. My dedication to running ultimately shaped both my future and the future of our cross-country team. I contributed by pushing my teammates and allowing them to push me in return. One piece of wisdom from my father that always stuck with me was, "Wherever you go, be sure to make history."

On the athletics website, the best times for every cross-country event were listed, with one of the most impressive 10 KM times set back in 1995. Each time I looked at that record, I couldn't help but wonder if I had what it took to surpass it. Achieving such a feat was no simple task, as every race had unique conditions, including elevation, weather, and practice. Setting a new record required immense dedication, effort, and perfect timing.

My opportunity came in 2011 at the Chile Pepper Invitational in Arkansas, a 10 KM race hosted by a Division I university. It was a high-profile event, and the course was renowned for its quality. The 15-hour drive to the competition left me feeling anxious. To cope with my nerves, I ate less, spoke less, and focused on calming activities such as listening to music and watching light-hearted movies on the bus.

The race was set to commence at 8 a.m. It was a major event, and the course was reputable and familiar. I was in peak physical condition, the elevation was optimal, and the weather conditions were favorable. To familiarize ourselves with the course, we took a tour upon our arrival the previous evening, running through it for orientation before the actual race. We also attended a meeting with the coach, during which we were assigned numbers and provided with electronic scoring chips. The entire process was highly professional and organized. We were advised to drink plenty of water to stay hydrated, and for the first time, I made a conscious effort to follow this recommendation. By the next morning, I felt fully hydrated and ready to take on the challenge.

On the day of the race, I opted for a light breakfast consisting of yogurt and fruit. It was a strategic choice, as I wanted to avoid eating too much and potentially throwing up during or after the race. The competition began promptly with the sound of the starting gun, and I took off with the determination of a runner embarking on their first and last race combined.

Although a 10-race is typically a lengthy affair, the intense competition made the time pass quickly. Throughout the first half of the race, I felt strong and maintained a steady pace. As the race progressed, I began picking up speed, closing in on taller and stronger competitors. I pushed my thin, nimble legs to their limits, racing toward the finish line with every ounce of energy I could muster.

I crossed the finish line with an impressive time of 31 minutes and 1 second, to the ecstatic cheers of my teammates who exclaimed, "You are the man, Kip!" and "You did it!" At that moment, I wasn't focused on breaking records; my sole ambition was to achieve my personal best time. I wanted to create a lasting memory, something that my future children could look up to and be proud of for years to come.

Even before the official results were announced, our coach was certain that a new record had been set that day. I was overjoyed upon realizing that I had shattered the previous record, which had stood untouched for several years, by a margin of one minute and a few seconds. For those unfamiliar with running, covering a 400-meter track takes approximately one minute, so you can imagine the incredible speed required to achieve such a feat. At that moment, I felt like a true hero, having surpassed a milestone that I had long been aspiring to reach.

This outstanding performance wasn't my only personal best. I also achieved the second-best time in New Mexico for an 8-race, clocking in at 25 minutes and 25 seconds.

Unfortunately, a persistent problem plagued my running career—I consistently suffered from serious injuries to my left leg at the peak of competitions. These recurring injuries always seemed to strike right before important events like conferences or regional championships, leaving me wondering how well I could have performed if I had been able to run injury-free throughout the entire season.

Despite the tremendous effort put forth by every team member, we consistently fell short of qualifying for the championships. The level of competition was fierce, and it often felt like there was an elusive element that our team was lacking. This constant struggle was a source of frustration not only for us athletes but also for our coach. There was nothing we could do but wait for the next year to start anew and strive for better results.

The off-season provided a welcome change of pace, as it meant we were free from practice for a few months. This allowed us to dedicate more time to our classwork and jobs, while also marking the start of the magical snowfall season. For me, the off-season became a much-anticipated break, offering a chance to recharge and refocus on both my academic and personal life.

Throughout my college experience, I encountered a mix of good and bad times that ultimately shaped me into a better person. I learned valuable lessons about interpersonal relationships, discovering how to get along with different people, and identifying those I should spend time with or avoid on campus. These experiences taught me the importance of discernment and not placing my trust in everyone blindly.

I had a couple of friends with whom I primarily interacted during classwork or when we happened to cross paths in the cafeteria or library. Though I enjoyed socializing, I didn't want to dedicate all my time to hanging out and having fun, given my busy schedule. When some friends questioned why I worked, I jokingly replied, "To buy a plane," as a way to lighten the mood. In reality, I was responsible for all my expenses and clothing, as I was navigating life independently.

During school breaks like spring break, Thanksgiving, or Christmas holidays, most students would return home to spend time with their families. However, I would always remain on campus, as the dorms would be closed for maintenance, making it impossible for anyone to stay there. Instead, we had the option of renting a room in one of the other dorms within the campus or staying with a host family, who were always welcoming and accommodating.

One of the highlights of these breaks was the opportunity to embark on road trips to visit friends in El Paso, Texas. I vividly recall a near-accident that occurred during one such trip. As we were driving, another car merged into our lane without using its turn signal, speeding along at over 80 mph. I wasn't the one behind the wheel, but in a moment of panic, I reflexively slammed my foot down, searching for the brake pedal. Of course, as a passenger, there were no brakes on my side, but my instincts kicked in nonetheless. Within seconds, our car's speed had dropped to 40 mph. It was a terrifying experience, especially considering the complex steps needed to slow down a manual vehicle.

Spending an extended period away from home made it easy to forget the familiarity of being surrounded by family and friends who spoke the same language and shared a similar sense of humor. The distance created a unique sense of isolation that, at times, seemed to intensify with each passing day.

My friend and I made concerted efforts to carve out time together between classes, hoping to enjoy meals and catch up on the happenings in each other's lives. Despite our best intentions, these plans often fell through due to other commitments, such as work or conflicting class schedules. To maintain our connection, we relied on texting and phone calls to stay in touch and keep the lines of communication open.

CHAPTER 12

SUMMER IN DURANGO

BESIDES THE ACADEMIC DEMANDS AND CROSS-COUNTRY, THE opportunity to enjoy all-year-round seasons was the best. As an international student who arrived in Durango during the fall season, I was greeted by a breathtaking tapestry of colors as the leaves on the trees transformed into vibrant hues of red, orange, and yellow. The mild weather, with average temperatures ranging from the mid-60s to the low-40s Fahrenheit, made it a comfortable time to explore the picturesque landscape.

The scenic San Juan Mountains served as a majestic backdrop to the city, enhancing the allure of Durango's natural beauty. Strolls through the historic downtown area were particularly enchanting as the trees lining the streets displayed their vibrant fall foliage. Venturing outside the city, I found an abundance of outdoor activities amidst stunning autumn scenery.

The Animas River, embellished with vibrant fall colors along its banks, offered a serene spot for picnics or leisurely walks. The numerous parks and hiking trails in the region provided ample opportunities to immerse myself in nature and witness the striking contrast of colorful trees against the bright blue Colorado sky.

During the summer season, Durango, nestled in the picturesque state of Colorado, experiences delightful weather characterized by warm temperatures and clear skies. With average highs reaching around 85 degrees Fahrenheit in July, the warmest month, it offers a welcoming escape from the intense heat often found in other regions. The Animas River, adorned with vibrant greenery along its banks, adds to the charm of Durango's natural beauty. Towering trees provide ample shade for picnics or strolls, as the gentle sounds of the river create a soothing symphony for all to enjoy. This idyllic setting, paired with mild weather, makes Durango an ideal destination for those seeking a rejuvenating summer retreat.

During a memorable summer, my colleague, a highly proficient driver, took it upon himself to introduce me to the world of driving. Despite my lack of experience behind the wheel, I was eager to embrace this opportunity to learn and grow. I had spent countless hours observing others on the road, inquiring about the meanings of various signs and the proper protocol for encountering law enforcement.

Under the patient guidance of my esteemed instructor, I thrived. His trusty manual transmission vehicle served as the perfect tool to hone my skills, transforming me into a confident driver within a matter of days. As a college student, this accomplishment was a significant milestone, and I couldn't help but proudly showcase my newly acquired driver's license to friends who had yet to master the art of driving themselves.

One summer, the host family invited us for a sponsored rafting trip down the river. While it was scary for non-qualified swimmers like myself, it was an event that you could not miss. When we showed up at the site, dressed in summer attire—shorts and somewhat waterproof shirts—we embarked on a thrilling rafting experience down the Animas River in Durango, Colorado. It was an exhilarating adventure filled with breathtaking scenery and cold water. As we navigated through the rushing rapids, we couldn't help but be captivated by the lush greenery along the riverbanks and the majestic mountains in the distance.

The icy cold water, flowing swiftly down the stream, added an invigorating element to the ride. My heart raced as the raft swiftly maneuvered through the challenging twists and turns of the river, expertly guided by seasoned professionals. As we traversed the Animas River, we were enchanted by the untouched beauty of the surrounding wilderness, feeling truly immersed in nature. This unforgettable rafting journey offered a perfect blend of excitement, serenity, and awe-inspiring views, making it an absolute must for adventure seekers visiting Durango, Colorado.

The sight of bears ambling around campus and casually traversing the streets was both enchanting and unnerving. These majestic creatures came in all shapes and sizes—from mama and papa bears to their curious cubs, all rummaging through trash bins in search of leftover treats. One particularly hair-raising encounter occurred during an extended run deep into Durango's wooded trails, renowned for hiking and mountain biking.

After approximately 30 minutes of vigorous running, I spotted a bear just 50 meters ahead. Thankfully, the wild animal remained oblivious to my presence, allowing me to swiftly retreat and ensure my safety. As I dashed away, I alerted others to the potential danger, although they seemed unfazed by the prospect of encountering a bear in the wild. This experience served as a stark reminder of the precarious balance between the wonders of nature and the inherent risks of venturing into the untamed wilderness.

My buddy and I often found ourselves securing housing jobs for two consecutive summers, and it was a good time. We assisted in arranging various summer camp events, which ranged from moving bunk beds around to debunking them when needed. We worked hard, but securing the job consecutively was challenging and competitive. Thanks to the housing criteria, which did not hire a few of us for the last two summers, this also turned out to be a blessing because it opened up a way to explore other rewarding job opportunities on campus to widen our experiences.

During my final two summers, I secured a job at the physical plant, where I had the privilege of meeting an extraordinary individual. This remarkable gentleman demonstrated unparalleled expertise in his paint shop, approaching his work with exceptional passion and dedication. As his mentee, I learned invaluable fundamentals of painting, which forever shaped my skills and perspective on the craft.

Each morning, he would gather us together to outline the tasks of the day, and it was impossible not to be motivated by his enthusiasm and genuine care for our growth. We were more than just coworkers; we were like an extended family, and his affectionate reference to us as "kids" evoked a comforting sense of nostalgia. His patient and precise teaching, from demonstrating how to professionally roll a brush on a wall to his warm praise for a job well done, made our learning experience truly enriching.

To this day, the skills he imparted remain with me, and I have never needed to hire a professional painter for any paint job, all thanks to the invaluable lessons he shared. My time working alongside this exceptional mentor in the physical plant department was a transformative experience, and I remain profoundly grateful for having crossed paths with such a remarkable individual.

One summer took a delicious turn when another Kenyan, a celebrated chef, graced us with his presence in Durango. This talented individual had traversed the globe, lending his culinary prowess to an array of countries and cruise ships. His versatility knew no bounds—he could effortlessly transform any ingredient into a mouthwatering dish. Yet, during his exceptional skills, I came to realize that perfection is not the ultimate goal; instead, it's the love and passion for one's craft that truly matters.

One unforgettable evening, a Kenyan coach hosted a cookout and storytelling gathering at his home, offering an opportunity for "men's talk." As the chef regaled us with tales in his native Swahili, we found ourselves questioning the effectiveness of our early school teachers, given his remarkable fluency. By the end of the night, we were so satiated that we opted to let someone else take the wheel, allowing our bellies a chance to digest the sumptuous feast.

CHAPTER 13

WINTER TRIP TO DENVER

Experiencing snow for the first time in Durango, I was captivated by the magical transformation of the landscape. The gentle descent of delicate snowflakes created a serene atmosphere, blanketing the city and its surroundings in a soft layer of white. The moment I stepped outside and felt the cold, powdery snow beneath my feet, I was completely immersed in a world unlike any I'd known before.

I was invited to my first snowball fight, along with sledding and all the other sports that come with it, but I always declined, fearing for the safety of my tiny legs. However, building a snowman became a new and delightful winter pastime as I embraced the unique opportunities that the snowy season offered. Navigating the snowy streets and sidewalks required some adjustments, as I learned to walk carefully on icy surfaces and bundle up in warm clothing to stay comfortable.

I remember an incident on campus when I decided to ride my bicycle on the icy sidewalk, eager to explore the snowy landscape. Suddenly, my tires lost traction, and I crashed to the ground with a jarring thud. Concerned passersby rushed to my aid, their worried faces revealing the dramatic nature of the scene. Thankfully, I only suffered minor scrapes and bruises, and the kind strangers helped me up, offering reassurance and advice for navigating the treacherous conditions. Their genuine concern was a reminder of the supportive community that surrounded me during my time as an international student. Although I never fully adapted to the winter season, my first experience with snow in Durango was a magical and unforgettable part of my journey.

In another memorable incident, the two of us inadvertently embarked on a winter expedition to Denver, Colorado. The primary catalyst for this journey was my Kenyan brother's acquisition of a Toyota Avalon, a vehicle that represented a dream come true. Both the price and condition of the car appeared favorable, and it became increasingly evident that having a second vehicle would significantly enhance our mobility and convenience.

Having explored Durango to our heart's content, we yearned to discover the charm of other cities and forge connections with their captivating residents. The acquisition of the Toyota Avalon symbolized our newfound ability to transcend Durango's boundaries, enabling us to delve deeper into the rich tapestry of cultures, stories, and landscapes that lay before us. The impending winter season only added to the thrill and anticipation of the experiences that awaited us.

Our journey commenced on a seemingly favorable morning, as the typical six-hour drive promised smooth sailing on snow-free roads. As we cruised along, the uplifting rhythms of our favorite reggae tunes filled the air, interspersed with lighthearted banter and peals of laughter.

My colleague took the lead, driving ahead of me as we maintained a safe distance between our vehicles. With his expertise in handling such conditions, I found myself relying on his tire tracks as a guide, trailing behind his every move. He would periodically slow down, allowing me to catch up, and our flip phones remained connected, enabling us to communicate and share vital information about the icy stretches of the road that lay ahead.

A colleague's advice on how to handle the vehicle when it began to slide proved invaluable. He emphasized the importance of avoiding sudden braking, as it could exacerbate the situation and increase the likelihood of skidding off the road. Armed with his guidance and maintaining a cautious approach, I managed to navigate the precarious conditions, successfully averting any further incidents that could have landed me off the road.

Upon reaching Wolf Creek Pass, we were awestruck by its breathtaking beauty. Perched at a lofty elevation of 10,857 feet, this mountain pass nestled within the San Juan Mountains of western Colorado is truly a sight to behold. However, navigating this route during the winter months can prove challenging, particularly for smaller vehicles like ours. Indeed, one would have to be daring—or perhaps a bit crazy—to attempt traversing Wolf Creek Pass in a Toyota Camry amidst the thick of winter.

As we ventured forth, the clear skies above did not indicate the impending snowfall. Undeterred, we pressed on, despite noticing that the majority of vehicles on the road were sturdy 4x4s, equipped with snow tires and hydraulic extraction devices. Little did we know that we were about to face the unforgiving power of nature head-on.

As the day wore on, we successfully sealed the deal for the Toyota Avalon, ecstatic about our purchase as college students. With the transaction complete, we set off on our return journey in the late afternoon with two vehicles, just as the first signs of snowfall began to descend. Undaunted by the deteriorating weather conditions, we pressed forward, only to realize that our small vehicle was attracting concerned glances from the drivers of sturdier automobiles.

As we approached Wolf Creek Pass, our perilous situation became all too apparent. The road was blanketed in a thick layer of snow, obscuring any indication of the middle line. I found myself losing control, skidding off the road not once, but twice. The treacherous conditions demanded that we maintain a slow and steady pace, clocking in at a meager ten miles per hour, effectively doubling our travel time.

Amidst the chaos, a kind gentleman came to our aid, pulling my vehicle back onto the road and offering valuable advice about staying in the middle to avoid further accidents. At one point, we decided to swap vehicles, hoping that the heavier one would provide more stability on the icy terrain.

With eyes fixed on the road, music silenced, and our sole focus on navigating what we could only hope was the middle of the road, we used the rails as a guiding beacon to lead us to safety. Through sheer determination and a healthy dose of luck, we emerged from our harrowing journey triumphant, forever grateful for the lessons learned and the extraordinary tale we lived to tell.

CHAPTER 14

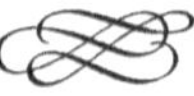

GROWING PAINS AND LASTING BONDS

THE FOUR YEARS OF COLLEGE SEEMED TO PASS BY IN A FLASH, and it was only when I found myself attending graduation ceremonies, and watching my friends cross the stage, that the reality of entering the "real world" began to sink in. Despite my initial doubts about completing a four-year degree, there I was, witnessing the fruits of my labor unfold before me.

In my third year, I started to loosen up and embrace the college town, finally feeling like an adult once again. This newfound comfort allowed me to cultivate deeper friendships, as people took me under their wings, showing me how to let loose and even teaching me a few dance moves. It was an exciting time of personal growth, exploration, and strengthening connections with those around me.

As my four-year college journey progressed, I found myself facing several challenges. My fourth year knocked on the door, yet I had not accomplished all the goals I had set for myself. One of my primary aspirations was to lead the cross-country team to the championships before completing my studies, but achieving this ambition proved to be immensely difficult. Despite the uncertainty, I was determined to work hard and make sacrifices in pursuit of this dream.

During my senior year, I experienced a significant setback when my head coach—the very person who had brought me to the college went on for bigger dreams. The loss hit me hard, as my mentor and dear friend were no longer by my side, and I was unsure about who would step in to fill this critical role. Eventually, I was introduced to my new head coach. I was somewhat familiar with him, having seen him around campus and at Durango High School, where he coached, and where we occasionally borrowed their field for practice.

It quickly became apparent that he was an excellent coach, as he had a no-nonsense approach and was unafraid to remove anyone from the team who wasn't putting in their best effort. With my final year of college and last chance to compete rapidly approaching, I felt compelled to give it my all and create lasting memories for both myself and my teammates. He once told me, "Hey man, I am counting on you," and even though I didn't know him well at the time, I took his words to heart and believed in his confidence in me.

As our practices continued, it was clear that the coach was pushing the team to new heights, and I began to believe that he was the key to fulfilling my wish of leading the cross-country team to the championships. My primary motivation for this goal was recognition; sports like soccer, basketball, and football seemed to overshadow cross-country, receiving most of the attention and praise from the college administration. I wanted to change that perception, showing that cross-country was more than just a means to stay fit and occupied. To achieve this, I knew the team had to reach the championship level to garner the attention it deserved.

Coach's coaching style like the previous one was demanding, and he began the season by taking us on a week-long training camp in the mountains. This intense experience not only allowed us to refine our skills but also provided an opportunity for the coach to instill a strong sense of determination and dedication within the team. Most of my teammates were either new or, like me, in their final year, which added a sense of urgency to our shared mission.

Balancing competition with my personal life proved challenging, as I was also nurturing a relationship and striving to maintain communication with my loved one. However, I remained unwavering in my commitment to the team and our goals. Although the training was more rigorous than in previous years, the methods employed by the coach were not entirely unfamiliar, as it seemed that most coaches shared a similar repertoire of drills and strategies.

The two assistant coaches were also familiar faces, with one being a previous teammate, who had already graduated, and the other being his friend. This camaraderie among the coaching staff fostered a sense of unity and mutual support, which further solidified our team's resolve to push ourselves beyond our limits.

Despite my dedication to the cross-country team, I wasn't always at the peak of my physical condition due to the numerous other responsibilities vying for my attention. Between working various jobs and enrolling in a hefty credit hour to satisfy the requirements for my degree, I was constantly occupied, striving to attain the highest grades possible to bolster my GPA. As a result, running became somewhat of a secondary focus, as my academic pursuits took precedence.

Nonetheless, I was able to navigate these challenges and succeed in my endeavors thanks to two key traits: flexibility and hard work. By learning to adapt to my ever-changing circumstances and maintaining a strong work ethic, I managed to stay afloat and make progress towards my goals. As they say, being in the right place at the right time, doing the right thing, was my guiding principle, like a song that kept me moving forward.

Throughout the monthly meets, our coach remained enthusiastic and optimistic, as he could see the potential for our team to reach the championships. However, I struggled to share his conviction, and it wasn't until the regional race in Denver, Colorado, that I began to believe in our team's chances of success. This race held a special significance for me as it was not only my final race before graduation but also marked the end of my eligibility to compete.

Regional races, being 10 kilometers long, are highly competitive events, serving as the selection grounds for the top five teams advancing to the championships. The stakes were high, and the atmosphere was tense, as every team and coach was determined to secure their spots. The course we faced in Denver was especially challenging—a hilly golf course with a higher elevation and the approaching winter adding to the difficulties.

Despite the obstacles we faced, I found myself in peak physical condition at this critical juncture, thanks to my relentless training regimen. In addition to the workouts prescribed by our coach, I had been going in extra mile to further enhance my endurance and strength. The fruits of my labor were evident, as I could now tackle hilly terrain with the same ease as I would flat surfaces, a feat that any runner can appreciate.

Running uphill can be an incredibly daunting task, especially when exhaustion sets in. For many, it feels like suffocating, with the brain being deprived of blood and oxygen and the lower legs gradually losing their strength. However, my rigorous training had prepared me for these very challenges, enabling me to push through the pain and maintain my focus on the race ahead.

As we took our positions at the starting line, I was acutely aware that this would be my final race, and I was determined to make it a memorable one. I scanned the crowd of competitors, keeping an eye out for familiar faces from Adams State University who had always given me a good challenge. There was one runner, in particular, with whom I had developed a friendly rivalry—gauging each other's performance at the end of each race and shaking hands in a show of sportsmanship. I knew if I crossed the finish line before him, I was performing well.

The race commenced with the blast of a whistle and a gunshot, and we took off in a tightly knit pack. I never particularly enjoyed the beginning of races, as the adrenaline and anticipation always left me feeling a mix of nerves, hunger, and the need to use the bathroom. Fortunately, my hydration was on point, and my experience had taught me how to strategize for a successful race.

As the first lap came to a close, the pack began to fragment, and runners started settling into their paces. My endurance training had paid off, as I still felt strong at this point. Seizing the opportunity, I decided to catch up with the group ahead. After a few minutes, the group began to slow down, prompting me to pursue the next batch of runners and pick up my speed.

At this point in the race, I estimated that I was within the top ten, although it was difficult to get an accurate count while in motion. To play it safe, I set my sights on a few more athletes ahead of me and attempted to close the distance between us. However, overtaking them proved to be a challenge, so I chose to remain just behind them and conserve my energy for the upcoming hilly section.

When we reached the hill, I unleashed all my power and sprinted as if I were running for my life—like escaping from a bear. I reminded myself of my ultimate goal: to qualify for the championship. Glancing behind me, I could barely spot my teammates; they were spread out across the course, and I wasn't sure if they could perform at the level I had hoped. Though I wasn't disappointed, I realized I needed to double my efforts to score as many points as possible for the team.

Qualifying for the championship as a group was undoubtedly more manageable, but I was prepared for either scenario. With that in mind, I focused on the race at hand and pushed forward with relentless determination. As the race progressed, I successfully surpassed around five competitors who had previously been ahead of me.

As the finish line came into view, I gave it my all and sprinted towards the end with every ounce of energy I had left. Making a sharp turn, I stretched my body as if crossing that line meant saving the world. The cheering from the crowd made the moment feel truly majestic, akin to the Olympics, though on a smaller scale. I completed the race with a time of 32 minutes and 20 seconds—perhaps not the fastest time for professional runners but certainly impressive for this particular course.

Finishing in seventh place, I secured a spot in the top ten and automatically qualified for the championship, even if the team didn't make it. We congratulated one another on our accomplishments, filled with a sense of camaraderie and hope for the overall results. The top ten individual runners were awarded medals, and I was proud to be among them. The feeling of accomplishment was indescribable.

Soon, the team rankings were announced. To our immense delight, we had secured the fifth position, which meant that the Fort Lewis cross-country team would be heading to the championships after several years of falling short. Our excitement was palpable as we cheered, took numerous pictures, and basked in the moment of success. Many of my teammates made phone calls to share the incredible news with their families, knowing that we would be representing our college at the championship.

CHAPTER 15

LAST RACE AND THE ROAD TO THE CHAMPIONSHIP

THE CHAMPIONSHIP WAS SET TO TAKE PLACE AT THE University of Tulsa, Oklahoma, in just two weeks. Our team embarked on a rigorous training regimen during this time, taking extra care to avoid any injuries that could jeopardize our performance. However, I found myself struggling as the extra effort I had exerted during the regional competition had aggravated a previous injury in my left lower leg.

Although I was all too familiar with this recurrence, I knew that my competitive running days were drawing to a close. I chose not to disclose my condition to the coach, fearing that it might dampen the team's spirit and morale. Instead, I decided to power through the discomfort, determined not to let my personal setback impact the team's collective drive to succeed in the championship.

As daily athletic training sessions continued, I found myself needing to scale back my efforts due to the worsening pain in my leg. I began to lag behind my teammates during the more strenuous workouts, but I kept the true severity of my injury hidden from everyone. To the coach, I downplayed it as a minor issue, but in reality, it felt as though my leg might break at any moment.

Despite the pain and the knowledge that my final race was fast approaching, I refused to give up. Deep down, I wished I could compete for an All-American title, but my physical limitations made that dream feel increasingly unattainable. However, the fact that I had already achieved one of my primary goals—qualifying for the championship—gave me some solace, knowing that I had left a lasting mark on the team's history.

During my time in the athletics room, I formed many friendships, primarily with football and soccer players who often visited for treatment. We bonded over our shared experiences and the challenges we faced as athletes, discussing our respective teams and personal struggles. For me, each interaction held special significance, as I was driven by the desire to leave a lasting legacy before moving on from this chapter of my life.

With graduation on the horizon, I knew my time at the college was limited. Soon, I would be packing up and embarking on the next journey, with the likelihood of returning only to visit close friends and family who resided in the area. This sense of impermanence made me all the more determined to make the most of my remaining time and create memories that would endure even after I was gone.

The day finally arrived, and we departed for the highly anticipated race in Tulsa, Oklahoma. There was an air of excitement among us as we traveled as a team, proudly donning our school-issued uniforms. The sense of fellowship was palpable, and I felt like a champion, ready to take on the challenge that lay ahead.

We took turns capturing the moment through photographs at the airport, relishing in the joy and anticipation of what was to come. Our journey even caught the attention of the local newspapers, and I could imagine the people of our hometown reading the articles and admiring the faces of the young men who were about to represent our college in the cross-country championship.

During our layovers at various airports, the team exuded an energetic and lively spirit, running up and down stairs, brimming with enthusiasm. However, my demeanor remained calm and collected, a stark contrast to my teammates' buoyant behavior. My injury had significantly hindered my mobility, making it difficult for me to even walk down the stairway. At this point, the prospect of running seemed like a distant memory.

Upon arriving at the hosting university for the championship, we were greeted by a crowd of fellow competitors representing their respective colleges and universities. The atmosphere was electric, reminiscent of the grandeur and excitement typically seen only on television. We were directed to our designated spot on the basketball court, and as we approached the sign bearing our college name, a vibrant and charismatic young boy wearing our team shirt eagerly awaited us.

His infectious energy and engaging demeanor instantly endeared him to us. He was to be our flag bearer, leading us onto the stage during the opening ceremony. This spirited encounter lifted our collective mood, and we couldn't help but share in his excitement as we prepared to take part in this momentous occasion.

As we marched onto the stage with our flag held high, I couldn't help but feel a profound sense of awe and wonder at the spectacle unfolding around us. At that moment, I wished that this championship wasn't my first and only experience—I longed for the opportunity to represent my college in this grand arena multiple times. The entire experience was truly awe-inspiring, and as we took our seats for the ceremony, I felt a renewed passion for athletics stir within me.

Surrounded by dedicated athletes and supportive spectators, the atmosphere was positively electric. It was as if we were participants in the Olympics, with the promise of a hard-earned medal hovering tantalizingly close. The ceremony, although relatively brief, was a heartwarming event. Each team was introduced, warmly welcomed, and congratulated on the achievements that had led them to the championship.

Once the ceremony concluded, we ventured into the local town in search of a well-deserved dinner. Our coach, always considerate and understanding, allowed us to choose our preferred dining locations and simply asked us to regroup at a designated meeting spot once our time was up. This freedom was a testament to the strong bond and mutual trust that had developed between us throughout our journey.

Upon returning to our hotel, we gathered for a brief meeting with our coach to discuss the race ahead and receive our respective chips and numbers. During the discussion, the topic of substitutions arose, particularly regarding a teammate who was on standby. The thought of asking him to run in my place crossed my mind, given the extent of my injury. However, deep down, I knew that despite the pain, I was still capable of delivering a strong performance. With the conviction that this was my final race, I resolved to push through my discomfort and give it my all on the course.

The morning of the race arrived, and it was clear that my teammates were in peak condition, ready to tackle the challenge ahead. In stark contrast, I found myself struggling, unable to partake in the usual warm-up routine due to the tightness and pain in my injured leg. It was as if my body sensed the impending race and was rebelling against me.

As the race commenced, I managed to maintain a solid pace for the first mile, but it soon became evident to my teammates that something was amiss. Typically, I would pull ahead and reconnect with them only at the finish line. This time, however, I verbally expressed my struggle to a teammate running close by, urging him to forge ahead without me. He promptly responded, increasing his speed, and the rest of the team followed suit, leaving me behind as they took on the remainder of the race.

I couldn't help but yearn for the ability to perform at the same level I had in previous competitions. A notable aspect of other teams was the presence of fellow Kenyan students who shared my height and had a similar build, though they were slightly more muscular. Their talent and leadership were undeniable, and they played an integral role in their team's success.

Despite my injury, I persevered and completed the race with a respectable time. However, the effort had taken its toll on my body, leaving me unable to walk to the finish line. In a display of comradeship and support, a teammate offered to carry me on his back, and I gratefully accepted his help. His lighthearted approach to the situation brought a smile to my face, and there was no way I could refuse such a genuine gesture of friendship.

As the race concluded and the results came in, it became clear that the team had performed exceptionally well, with many of my teammates achieving their personal best times. Sadly, I was unable to capitalize on the perfect conditions—the ideal elevation, favorable weather, intense competition, and a course that was tailor-made for record-breaking performances. Nonetheless, as we departed Oklahoma, tears of joy streamed down my face. I had accomplished the very reason I had chosen Fort Lewis —to help restore the cross-country team to its former glory.

Our success in Oklahoma had revitalized the cross-country program, and the coach, beaming with pride, encouraged us to consider participating in track and field events as well. However, my time at Fort Lewis was drawing to a close, and I had no intention of joining the track and field team. Though I enjoyed watching the events, I lacked the desire and energy to undertake another season of competition, especially with the demands of my academic coursework and part-time job already weighing on me.

In recognition of my dedication and contribution to the team's success, Coach Carson presented me with the Most Valuable Player award. His heartfelt speech about my perseverance in the face of adversity, as well as my commitment to attending daily treatment sessions for my injury, deeply moved me. Receiving this award was an exhilarating moment, especially as it signaled the end of my running career and the relentless cycle of injuries that had plagued me throughout my journey.

With this chapter of my life coming to a close, I was both relieved and eager to embrace the new challenges that awaited me. As I stepped away from the world of competitive running, I knew that my experiences at Fort Lewis had not only prepared me for life beyond college but also instilled in me the determination and resilience necessary to face the real world head-on.

As my final semester unfolded, I found myself with a relatively light course load, having already fulfilled the requirements for my Public Health degree. With only two mandatory classes left, the remainder of my schedule was filled with electives aimed at boosting my grade. This newfound flexibility meant that I no longer had to dedicate as much time to attending classes and studying in the library.

Instead, I chose to invest my newfound free time in other important aspects of my life, such as increasing my work hours and initiating the search for post-college employment. Contrary to popular belief, securing a job after graduation proved to be quite challenging. Not only was it difficult to find positions that aligned with my area of specialization, but my lack of experience further limited my prospects, forcing me to consider roles that were less than ideal.

Despite these obstacles, I remained steadfast in my pursuit of the perfect opportunity, determined to leverage the valuable skills and knowledge gained during my time at Fort Lewis to carve out a fulfilling and rewarding career path.

As my college journey neared its conclusion, it became abundantly clear just how much I had grown and evolved since first setting foot on campus. My understanding of the world had expanded dramatically, and I now possessed a wealth of knowledge that I had been previously unaware of. This newfound wisdom also granted me the ability to discern true friends from those who were less genuine, as well as the capacity to differentiate between what was legal and what was not.

Armed with a college degree and a well-rounded set of skills, I felt confident that I was well-prepared to face whatever challenges lay ahead. The transformations I had undergone throughout my college years had left me a more proficient writer, an eloquent speaker, and a decisive individual. It was evident that I was ready to venture out into the world on my own and make the most of the opportunities that awaited me, driven by the desire to carve out a successful and fulfilling future for myself.

CHAPTER 16

EMBRACING FREEDOM AND SERVICE

GRADUATING FROM COLLEGE AND LEAVING ACADEMIA BEHIND brought with it a sense of liberation that was difficult to describe. Gone were the days of adhering to a class schedule, listening to professors debate the merits of philosophy, or engaging in arguments about the existence of nature and the age-old question of whether the chicken or the egg came first. No longer burdened by homework assignments or the pressures of adhering to strict academic timetables, I reveled in the newfound freedom afforded to me as a fresh college graduate.

With a car at my disposal and some financial savings to fall back on, I felt empowered to embark on the next chapter of my life without the immediate pressure to secure employment. This temporary respite was a luxury I could afford, thanks in part to the NCAA support that saw me through my college career.

Despite my newfound independence, I couldn't help but reflect on the family I had left behind over four years ago.

Though we remained in regular contact, exchanging well-wishes and updates on our respective lives, the distance between us served as a constant reminder of my humble beginnings and the unchanged lifestyle awaiting me back home. These thoughts never strayed far from my mind, fueling my determination to forge a successful path and prove that I could rise above the circumstances of my past.

As I contemplated my post-college plans, I found myself grappling with the concerns of others regarding my future. Coming from a country with a turbulent history and a challenging economic landscape, it was difficult to provide a clear answer to any inquiries. With only a college degree to my name, and lacking both experience and financial resources, I prepared to face the challenges that lay ahead.

However, I recognized that my unique background and firsthand experience with my country's customs and traditions had granted me a valuable perspective. This understanding fueled my desire to empower the next generation, encouraging them to pursue their dreams and strive for a better future. The dire reality of rising unemployment rates, even among those with advanced degrees, further emphasized the need for careful decision-making.

Amidst the uncertainty, I remained steadfast in my belief that the opportunities I had been afforded were not merely a matter of luck. Instead, I saw them as blessings, and I felt a deep sense of responsibility to make the most of them. With this in mind, I knew that giving up was not the answer. I was determined to leverage my education and newfound skills to create positive change and serve as a beacon of hope for those facing similar challenges.

As a recent college graduate, I found myself standing at the precipice of an uncertain future, grappling with the daunting challenges that lay ahead. The excitement of earning my degree was quickly overshadowed by the realization that I lacked the experience and financial resources necessary to secure a stable job. Despite these hurdles, I was determined to rise to the occasion. With a steadfast resolve, I embraced the challenge of finding meaningful opportunities that would not only provide me with valuable experience but also allow me to inspire the next generation. I knew that every obstacle I faced was a stepping stone toward something bigger, and I was ready to navigate this uncharted territory with perseverance and hope.

With an undergraduate degree in hand, I was acutely aware of the harsh reality that countless friends from my village, some even holding graduate degrees, still struggled to secure employment. In my eyes, my bachelor's degree was merely an addition to my high school diploma, and I knew that further education, experience, and growth were necessary to truly distinguish myself in the job market.

Having invested a significant amount of time and resources into my college education, I felt a strong sense of duty to give back to the nation that had provided me with invaluable knowledge and opportunities. By working and paying taxes, I believed that I could make a meaningful contribution to the country that had supported my academic journey.

As I began my job search, I quickly realized that securing a position in my field without prior experience was an uphill battle. I submitted numerous applications, only to be met with silence or rejection. To my dismay, I discovered that I didn't even qualify for an environmental specialist role—essentially a janitorial position—at a local organization. It was disheartening to be deemed unqualified for a cleaning job at a nearby hospital, simply because I lacked relevant experience and references.

Feeling the pressure to find any legal means of earning an income, I refused to give up. Eventually, my persistence paid off when I landed a cleaning job with a private company near La Plata County Airport. While I was not directly employed by an organization, I found it more convenient to tell curious acquaintances that I worked for the company. This simplified explanation allowed me to avoid delving into the details of my actual position and helped me gauge whether the inquirer had an ulterior motive for their interest in my occupation.

Eventually, it became crucial for me to balance two jobs to meet my basic living expenses. My first job offered a mere 25 hours per week, which proved insufficient to cover both housing and gas costs. At the end of each exhausting day, I would immediately transition to my second job, which ran from 5:30 p.m. to 10:30 p.m. This grueling schedule left little time for rest and rejuvenation before starting the cycle anew the next morning.

As the relentless routine of working, commuting, and snatching moments of respite took its toll, it also catalyzed self-reflection. I began to contemplate the prospect of a better life and recognized the crucial role that furthering my education could play in improving my circumstances. The challenges I faced during this demanding period ultimately fueled my ambition and determination to create a brighter future for myself.

To make this challenging period more manageable, I steered clear of any illegal activities or unhealthy habits that could potentially derail my progress. Avoiding drinking and gambling helped me stay focused and made my life considerably easier. In retrospect, I can confidently say that maintaining this level of discipline and determination was instrumental in getting me through those tough times and laying the groundwork for my future success.

Amid life's daily stresses, my partner and I discovered a sanctuary in the picturesque Serious Texas BBQ South Durango. Nestled along the tranquil Animas River, this idyllic barbecue spot provides the perfect retreat for couples seeking solace in nature's beauty. The gentle sound of the flowing river and the mouthwatering aroma of expertly cooked beef created an irresistible allure, satisfying Raven's cravings and leaving us spellbound.

Time and again, we found ourselves returning to this haven, enticed by the enchanting surroundings and delectable cuisine. The unforgettable ambiance and flavors of Serious Texas BBQ South Durango never failed to provide us with the respite we needed from the hustle and bustle of everyday life.

Nearby, a cluster of shopping centers piqued our interest, particularly a military recruiting office that seemed to stand out from the rest. After several visits to Durango, my curiosity finally got the better of me, and I decided to step inside the quiet office. I braced myself, half-jokingly wondering if I'd be arrested for simply entering the space.

Several of my dear friends had already embarked on the noble journey of serving in the Army. However, the thought of joining their ranks had never occurred to me due to my physique—both my height and weight seemed to pose insurmountable obstacles. This self-doubt stemmed from the stringent physical criteria set forth by the Kenya Defense Forces, which had inadvertently instilled within me a mindset that deemed me unfit for service.

Consequently, the possibility of enlisting in the service felt like an unattainable dream, as I had been led to believe that my physical attributes were a hindrance rather than an asset. I found myself grappling with the constraints imposed by these stringent requirements, which appeared to quash any hope of pursuing a military career alongside my cherished friends.

The room suddenly reverberated with a resounding proclamation: "You can't be a Marine!" The authoritative Marine Sergeant had made his opinion known, yet his words failed to dampen my spirits. As I surveyed the scene, my gaze fell upon a tall, distinguished figure—Navy personnel, his piercing blue eyes inviting me to join him for a conversation. Another sailor, an affable and hardworking man, sat beside him, his fingers nimbly navigating the computer keyboard. Both men were impeccably attired in their camouflage uniforms, their boots glistening from a meticulous polish.

As I stole a glance toward the exit, my attention was drawn to the American, Navy, Army, and Marine flags that stood united. At that moment, the powerful symbolism of these emblems stirred within me a deep sense of gratitude for the liberties and prospects that this great nation had to offer. Regardless of the Marine Sergeant's discouraging remark, the presence of these flags served as an unwavering reminder of the boundless opportunities that awaited those who dared to dream.

Fast-forward to the present, and here I am, donning the same uniform as I serve as a Hospital Corpsman in the United States Navy. I'm proud to be giving back to this beautiful nation while supporting the courageous men and women who dedicate their lives to preserving the very freedom that has allowed me to pursue my dreams.

God Bless America

ABOUT THE AUTHOR

Kiprono Mutai is a distinguished alumnus of Kabusare High School and a former student-athlete from Fort Lewis College in Durango, Colorado. He majored in Public Health and graduated in 2013. Originally from Bomet, Kenya, Kip was an accomplished cross-country runner for the Fort Lewis College Skyhawks.

While at Fort Lewis, Mutai achieved significant milestones, including setting the school record for the 10k distance at 31:01.87. He was named the Most Valuable Player for the men's cross-country team and led the team to various top finishes in regional and national competitions. Notably, he was part of the team that placed 23rd at the NCAA Division II National Championships 2012.

Mutai's influence extended beyond his athletic achievements. His cheerful personality and strong work ethic were not just admired but highly valued by his teammates and coaches. His legacy at Fort Lewis College is not just about his records, but also about the positive impact he had on the college community.

www.ingramcontent.com/pod-product-compliance
Lightning Source LLC
Chambersburg PA
CBHW031736150726
47989CB00006B/2484